To The
Arnolds,
Those were the days!

Greg Marecek
Mo. HOF '86

The St. Louis Hawks

PRESS

ST. LOUIS HAWKS BASKETBALL CLUB, INC.

1960-61 **SEASON**

ARTHUR WHITMAN – POST PHOTOS

NON-TRANSFERABLE

Marty Blake

164

MARTY BLAKE, PUBLICITY DIRECTOR

Enter Thru 15th Street Stage Door

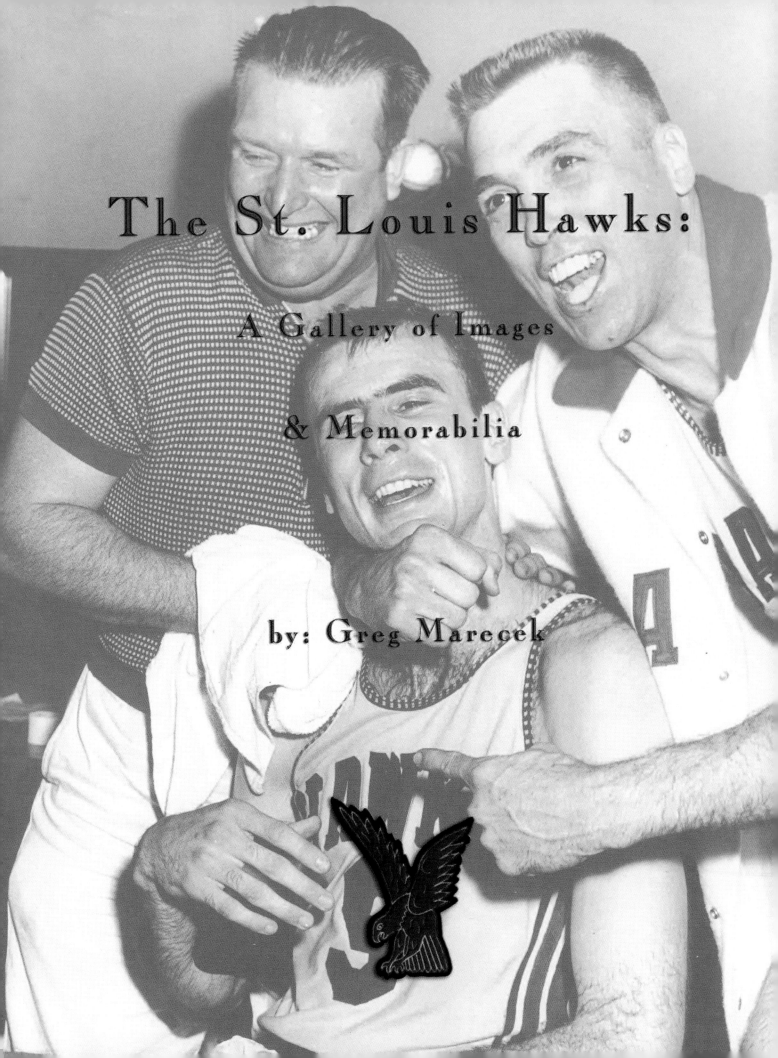

The St. Louis Hawks:

A Gallery of Images

& Memorabilia

by: Greg Marecek

Reedy Press
PO Box 5131
St. Louis, MO 63139

Design and Image Restoration Copyright © 2007 by William Mathis & Ellie Jones, MathisJones Communications, LLC,
1 Putt Lane, Eureka, Missouri, 63025, please contact MathisJones Communications at info@mathisjones.com

Library of Congress Cataloging-in-Publication Data: 2007934940

ISBN: 978-1-933370-15-6

For all information on all Reedy Press publications visit our Web site at http://reedypress.com.

Printed in the United States of America
07 08 09 10 11   5 4 3 2 1

Cover Photo by, Paul Okrassa, St. Louis Globe-Democrat Photography

Memoribilia photography, Copyright © 2007, by William E. Mathis

Contents

PREFACE

The Hawks left so many lasting memories because they weren't a humdrum team that didn't perform. Instead, they were a highly successful franchise on the court, which is what makes their story such a sad anomaly in all of sports history. How many sports teams in America changed cities after 13 years that included 12 playoff appearances, 10 Conference Finals, four NBA Finals, and one World Championship? The answer is one—these St. Louis Hawks.

Bring up the Hawks to a St. Louisan over the age of 50, and you'll get a story. These fan stories have become the most treasured aspects of reliving the era of the Hawks.

When jogged to remember the Hawks while collecting his baggage at the St. Louis Airport, St. Louis auto dealer giant Lou Fusz, Jr., beamed, "I was a ball boy for the Hawks. Those were fun days."

When presented with a copy of *Full Court: The Untold Stories of the St. Louis Hawks* during spring training in Jupiter, Florida, St. Louis Cardinals' Hall-of-Fame second baseman, No. 2, "The Old Redhead," Red Schoendienst told a great story:

"I was a youngster trying to stick with the Cardinals' minor league teams in 1946 when I got a big break. The shortstop the Cards were high on, who was playing at the Triple A level in Rochester, N.Y., got injured and I was told to go and replace him. After that, I earned the right to stay in St. Louis and never came back down again. Who was that shortstop who's bad luck was my good luck? Try the name Buddy Blattner, the voice of the Hawks!"

Kim Tucci is a well-known St. Louisan whose civic prominence and delicious Pasta House Company dishes are known across the city landscape. Before there was pasta in Tucci's life, however, he studied as a trainer and eventually took a job with the St. Louis Hawks. Tucci remembers:

"In college at Saint Louis University, I decided one day that running for miles in cross country and taking long car rides to meets wasn't for me and the late great Bob 'Doc' Bauman, the team trainer for SLU and the Cardinals, gave me first-hand instruction. I even got a scholarship in team training my senior year. The Hawks' trainer Bernie Ebert was dying of cancer, so Doc Bauman got me the job as trainer for the Hawks for two seasons, 1965–66 and 1966–67. By this time, I was teaching and coaching at DeAndreis High School."

The Pasta Baron recalls the kindly nature of the NBA's towering and intimidating giant, 7-1 Wilt the Stilt Chamberlain of the San Francisco Warriors. The game's most prolific scorer was truly a gentle giant. "You were in awe around Chamberlain, but he was truly a nice man," said Tucci. "I could count on Chamberlain coming to me every time we played the Warriors to ask for two band aids. What for? The uniform shirt he wore would so irritate his nipples he would wear the band aids for comfort. That was the mighty Wilt Chamberlain."

Tucci was honored to work the locker room of the Eastern Division squad coached by Boston Celtic Coach Red Auerbach when St. Louis hosted the 1965 East-West NBA All-Star Game at the St. Louis Arena.

Another story comes from a retiree in the financial investment industry, John Edwards, a lifelong St. Louisan, who as a small boy crossed paths with the greatest Hawk, Bob Pettit, one day. His story was typical of the stories told consistently about the Hawks' players' relationship with the community.
Pettit took notice of the young Edwards and asked him if he'd like to go downtown with Bob to Kiel Auditorium to see the rest of the team. The

speechless youngster spit out a "sure!" After getting proper permissions, Pettit put him in his car and headed to practice. At Kiel, John Edwards' eyes grew large as he walked onto the Kiel court and hung out with all the Hawks at a pregame practice! Then he watched the Hawks battle the Boston Celtics as guest of the team!

Edwards today is still in awe of being there with all the Hawks on a game day, and he has had a lifelong admiration for Bob Pettit as a kind gentleman who took the time to give a youngster the memory of a lifetime.

The media pressures and demands from the fans were vastly different in the 1950s and 1960s. Players welcomed the attention because it wasn't overbearing, and they certainly weren't "overpaid prima donnas." There was a bond, an understanding between the players and the fans that was genuine and not driven by dollars. The Hawks had saddled up side-by-side with the baseball Cardinals as "the pride of St. Louis."

Greg J. Marecek

Greg J. Marecek

When the Hawks are ON THE GO

Greg Marecek's first book, *Full Court: The Untold Stories of the St. Louis Hawks,* brought our story back to life for all the people who didn't remember us or never knew us. We players learned things we didn't know and had never put into perspective until stepping away from the game now many years later. What it did remind us of was the wonderful time we had playing in the National Basketball Association for owner Ben Kerner's Hawks. It made me laugh to read the comedy that was my first contract negotiation with Mr. Kerner, who by the way, I came to appreciate and admire for what he survived and accomplished for the Hawks and professional basketball.

The return to the limelight and the renewed adulation of the St. Louis basketball fans has been a heartwarming experience for myself and particularly for those players still residing in the St. Louis area, Easy Ed Macauley, Charlie Share, Al Ferrari, Coach Harry Gallatin, and others like Bud Blattner, Dr. Stan London, and of course, the charming wife of our owner, Mrs. Jean Kerner. After an exciting college basketball career at Louisiana State U., the state of affairs in my first year in Milwaukee for the Hawks was dreadful and without much promise. However, our instant success in St. Louis and our run for the World Championship in 1958 fulfilled all of our lifetime dreams in professional basketball.

"It made me laugh to read the comedy that was my first contract negotiation with Mr. Kerner"

Just when I thought it was time to get back to the quiet routine of a senior citizen who used to play basketball, our determined friend and author Greg Marecek has put out this magnificent book full of on- and off-the-court pictures and Hawks memorabilia, bound together with the written word to describe the images. Believe me, as players we have never seen most of the images in this book and find it a joy to relive these moments in our lives with the readers. Although, I'm not sure I needed to see the pictures of my broken wrist again that kept me out of games in the championship season. However, as Ed Macauley reminded me on this wonderful CD that is enclosed, getting hurt in February of 1957 may have been a blessing in disguise. I certainly came back with well-rested legs and a fresh outlook on the stretch run and ultimately the championship series.

Just looking at the advertisements from the game programs pictured in this awesome encyclopedia of the Hawks era brings back memories. The Wabash Railroad ad—which shows me, Coach Alex Hannum, Al Ferrari, and Med Park carrying our suitcases wearing coat and ties, heading for the train—brings back those long rides to Boston, New York, Minneapolis, and the other cities. Those overnights were particularly memorable. The big guys like Charlie Share and I had the struggle of getting comfortable enough to sleep in the train cars.

I had the pleasure of playing with a number of great NBA players, such as Cliff Hagan, Ed Macauley, Charlie Share, Slater Martin, Lenny Wilkens, and others too many to name.

One of the things I do remember were all the great players I had the pleasure of playing with and against. The section titled, "Colorful Characters and Fan Favorites" is particularly entertaining because it gives credit to the players who didn't necessarily make headlines every night. Who remembers Win Wilfong's tremendous contributions in 1957–58, right up to his championship clinching rebound in Game 6 with less than a half minute to play? Jack McMahon's floor leadership was crucial, and that two-handed set shot kept the defense honest. Finally, all of us have stories to keep you entertained about our general manager Marty Blake.

As to "NBA Stars Who Played Against the Hawks," the chapter about the other NBA stars we played against, this well-done piece really depicts the high quality of the pro game and truly entitles the 1950s and 1960s to be called the NBA's "Golden Era." Our battles with Bill Russell, Bob Cousy, Tom Heinsohn, and all of those incredibly tough Boston Celtics games are represented. We went from empty arenas to standing-room-only crowds based on the competitiveness of the two best teams of the times, us and Boston. Fans could come out and see the fantastic "Big O," Oscar Robertson, who could have coined the phrase "triple-double," which he achieved more times than any player in past or modern history! What a shooter and passer.

There wasn't a night off in the NBA of those days. You couldn't coast with Elgin Baylor, Jerry West, and the Los Angeles Lakers, who later created their own dynasty, or the sight of Wilt "The Stilt" Chamberlain posting those incredible point totals. The fans may have enjoyed it, but I can tell you it

-got old watching him score 50 or 60 points against you all the time. Imagine a 50-points-per-game average in an NBA season today? Not likely, but Wilt did it.

Well, you know everybody asks what it felt like to score those 50 points in the championship game in 1958, but all I can say is I knew I was scoring a lot of points, and they just kept going in. All I knew at the time was that I wanted badly to win that game. I knew we couldn't risk going back to Boston to try for a third road win in the series. I'm just thankful it happened, and by the way, Ed Macauley, I want to thank him for scoring two points that night so we could win, 110–109!

This book adds an incredible piece to St. Louis sports history right down to the beautiful color shots of all that memorabilia that for the life of me I don't remember seeing. Then the CD of the long -lost Buddy Blattner play by play is chilling to hear and surely is a classic discovery for players and fans. We thank you Buddy for keeping that tape all these 50 years! Greg, this treasure of a book is a three-point play.

—Bob Pettit

PROFESSIONAL
BASKETBALL
MAGAZINE AND PROGRAM

BOMBERS

ST·LOUIS

at the **ST·LOUIS ARENA** · Season **1948-49**

1 THE PROS COME TO ST. LOUIS

In June 1946, St. Louis had a taste of professional basketball with the Bombers in the Basketball Association of America (BAA), made up of member cities New York, Chicago, Boston, Philadelphia, Toronto, Detroit, Washington, Providence, Cleveland, Pittsburgh, and St. Louis. The Bombers played four seasons in near obscurity despite finishing one game out of the division title in 1946–47, being Western Division champions in 1947–48, and adding local star Ed Macauley, a two-time college All-American from Saint Louis University's national championship team, for the 1949–50 season.

The Bombers were a colorful lot. A second local player, D. C. Wilcutt, also from SLU, got playing time, along with Red Rocha and Johnny Logan, who survived a merger of leagues and played in the National Basketball Association. But even Macauley's team-leading 16 points per game couldn't stop the Bombers from tumbling into last place with a miserable 26–42 record, some 25 games behind the Central Division leaders.

While some members of the league thrived, others were failing. So the strongest franchises of each competing league, the NBA and the BAA, combined to become today's NBA. The Bombers were eliminated in St. Louis, losing the St. Louis Arena stockholders $146,000 over the four years. The Bombers, however, gave St. Louisans a taste of pro basketball, which helped the city get another team five seasons later. Picking up the game ball in St. Louis, the NBA Hawks were also a cellar dweller transferring from Milwaukee.

The owner was Ben Kerner, a hard-working promoter/salesmen of Jewish descent who had only one business interest—his beloved Hawks. Kerner's failures in Milwaukee weren't for lack of effort and were ultimately blessings for St. Louis. Five straight last-place finishes in Wisconsin combined to drive the Hawks south with a phenomenal superstar in tow. The inventive owner Kerner and future Hall of Famer Bob Pettit strolled down Market Street and into Kiel Auditorium.

East Coast writers decried the move, citing the city's loss of the BAA Bombers, not to mention pro hockey's St. Louis Flyers and Major League Baseball's St. Louis Browns. "A lousy sports

The wiley, gutsy owner of the Hawks Ben Kerner, a true pioneer of the NBA, brought his Milwaukee club to St. Louis in 1955.

Coach Paul Seymour is interviewed by Lindsey Nelson as Ben Kerner nervously waits his turn.

St. Louis Globe-Democrat *Sports Editor Bob Burnes gives Bob Pettit a sports magazine award.*

town" was the moniker labeling the Missouri River town. Kerner had decided to hang his hat on an Ash Wednesday success, a game transferred from Milwaukee to the St. Louis Arena in March 1955 when his St. Louis Hawks and Boston Celtics drew 8,000 curious fans.

That game–plus the well-meaning badgering by *St. Louis Globe-Democrat* Sports Editor Bob Burnes to give his city a chance and bring the Hawks here– was enough for the gambler in Mr. Kerner. The final acid test was a one-month trial to pre-sell 1,000 season tickets in St. Louis before making a franchise transfer decision, and when City Fathers bought 633 tickets in three weeks, that was enough. The Hawks were coming. The NBA voted unanimously on May 11, 1955, to transfer the beleaguered Milwaukee Hawks to St. Louis to begin play in the 1955–56 basketball season.

Buddy Blattner, superstar Bob Pettit, and guard Jack McMahon look over some material in the locker room before a game.

2 BEN KERNER'S HAWKS ARRIVE

Cinderella came to St. Louis and the party lasted thirteen glorious seasons. They'd been pro basketball vagabonds, from Buffalo to Tri-Cities to Milwaukee to St. Louis. They began as Blackhawks, then trimmed to just "Hawks," but few took note of this cellar dweller team.

When their carriage pulled up to their new home at Kiel Auditorium on May 11, 1955, they were virtually unnoticed, save for the 633 who'd bought season tickets on the come as a sign of faith to the Hawks' near-bankrupt owner Ben Kerner. Could

basketball make it for a second go around in St. Louis, which had lost the professional Bombers five years before?

The St. Louis Hawks became reality and answered the question with a resounding "YES!" They could, and they would, and they did turn into Cinderella. The St. Louis Chamber of Commerce knew their value. They filled a big void in the sports calendar. They ignited a new spark of civic interest and pride as their fame spread.

Hawks owner Ben Kerner and Cardinals owner Gussie Busch share a laugh while wearing Cardinals baseball hats after Anheuser-Busch became the new exclusive beer sponsor of Hawks games.

5

A classic shot of Buddy Blattner (left) alongside his broadcaster color man Dizzy Dean (right) during an NBC Major League Baseball Game of the Week telecast. They were baseball's first national telecast broadcasters.

Cliff Hagan takes one of his patented hook shots over the Lakers' Elgin Baylor.

A chamber executive of the day proclaimed, "The spirit the Hawks has engendered, and the fresh image of St. Louis they have molded is invaluable to the city and our reputation nationwide."

Make no mistake, that "spirit of the Hawks" was the result of an innovative promoter who didn't need stockholders, a board of directors, or another business to fund his exciting sports entity. Ben Kerner was part of the scene, the boss, the man who had the enterprise and the energy to hang in there during tough times and celebrate the victories, of which there were many.

Kerner had some outstanding assistance from the man he chose to saddle up as his public relations director/general manager, whose role as a talent scout and designer of arena promotions cannot be overlooked or underestimated. Marty Blake was involved in everything but signing the contracts, and many give Blake credit for being the pioneer of basketball talent scouting. This

twosome turned a dreadful team from Milwaukee into the Western Division's most powerful ball club for the first half-dozen seasons in the Gateway City.

Indeed, the positive image added by the Hawks to the already-imbedded tradition of the St. Louis Cardinals was being received everywhere through priceless newspaper, radio, and TV coverage. Having more than one professional sports team, and at that another winning team, added immeasurably to the status of St. Louis. The Hawks clearly showed the way for the Chicago Cardinals to complete their move to St. Louis and for the National Hockey League to okay a new franchise to begin operation.

The Hawks played with spirit from day one, and save one sorry season, they played their way into the hearts of the fans through twelve playoff seasons. There was no stereotyping a Hawks fan. For men and women alike, from the twenties to the seniors,

Slater "Dugie" Martin

Hawks team from 1955–56, the first season they advanced to the NBA Finals. Kneeling: Bob Feidhaus (mascot). First row, L to R: Charlie Share, Jack Coleman, Al Ferrari, Bob Schafer, Alex Hannum, Bob Pettit. Second row, L to R: Bob Scanlon, trainer; Marty Blake, publicity director; Bob Harrison, team captain; Med Park, Jack McMahon, Jack Stephens, William (Red) Holzman, Coach.

in gray flannel suits and factory jeans, winter's cold was tempered by "hot" Hawks basketball.

The NBA of the 1950s and 1960s had a much different feel than basketball today. It was a game where technique and teamwork were themes. Hawks fans marveled at the deft ball handling of hard-nosed guard Slater "Dugie" Martin and the silky moves through the lane for a patented hook shot by crowd favorite Cliff Hagan.

Basketball was playmaking, one-handed set shots, two-handed set shots, and underhanded free throws. The ball was never dunked, as Bob Pettit remarked: "Anyone who would try to dunk the ball could count on getting clobbered in the lane. It just wasn't done."

Scoring was prolific with games going over the 100-point mark for each team almost every night. It wasn't that unusual to see both teams over 120 points, and those 130- and 140-point nights were truly exciting. The players of the day were better shooters and, in particular, far better free throw shooters.

One January night in 1960, the Hawks poured in 155 points against the New York Knickerbockers (never called the Knicks) in a regulation game. On the flipside, St. Louis took a beating from the Philadelphia Warriors, giving up 147 points at Philly in 1961. The player who scored the most points in a game against the St. Louis Hawks was, no surprise, Wilt the Stilt Chamberlain, who thrilled Kiel fans with 67 points in February 1962. So which Hawk scored the most points in a game in team history? Need one ask—Big Blue Bob Pettit, with a 57-point barrage against the Detroit Pistons in the Motor City, also in 1961.

But the spirit of the Hawks was much more than the often-memorable performances of Pettit and Hagan. Throughout the thirteen seasons, there were many players who had crowd-pleasing styles. Whether it'd be a darting ballerina or a locomotive barreling down the lane, those wearing the

glistening white uniforms with red and blue with "Hawks" written across the chest were adored by women and envied by men.

Buddy Blattner's golden voice on the radio broadcasts was truly responsible for the images of the players in the minds of St. Louis fans. His wonderful habit of creating nicknames for the players brought them even closer to their fans. At a time when television was in its infancy, the call of the Hawks games by the great Blattner conjured visions in the minds of hungry fans of St. Louis basketball.

ST. LOUIS HAWKS

35¢

1955-56 EDITION

Pettit battles "Satch" Sanders (16), with Bill Russell in pursuit.

3   The Rivalry that Propelled the NBA

Before the Hawks even thought of moving to St. Louis, an NBA team played some games in the city, prospecting interest in the fledgling basketball league. Maybe this game added to what became the greatest NBA rivalry of the times. Yes, the Boston Celtics had played games in St. Louis before the Hawks ever showed up!

So, as unfamiliar as the St. Louis fans were with the NBA in general in 1955, they had at least seen the Kelly green of the Celtics when they played the first regular-season game in what would be a storied rivalry. On December 2, 1955, Boston handled the Hawks, 94–81, at Boston Garden and then again took it to St. Louis, 122–99, four days later in the first game at Kiel Auditorium.

As bad as that start was, the Hawks quickly turned it around, winning six of the next eleven meetings against Boston the rest of the first season. Bostonians still consider the April 13, 1957, game against the Hawks the most intense and electrifying game in history. The Celtics won that dramatic game in the 1956–57 NBA Finals 125–123 in double overtime. Historians say this series ignited the rivalry and rocketed the professional game of basketball into the national spotlight.

In thirteen seasons, Boston dominated the series in the Boston Garden with a 36–6 winning record, but on the road in St. Louis the Celtics had to fight for their lives. Fifty games were played at Kiel, and the Hawks battled the almost

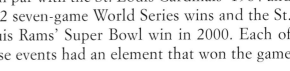

perennial NBA Champion Celts to a dead even 25 wins and 25 losses.

As poorly as the Hawks performed in regular-season games at The Garden, they were ferocious in postseason play. It began with the shocking 125–123 overtime upset of the Celtics in Game 1 of the 1956–57 Championship Series as overwhelming underdogs. After all, the Celtics had finished 16 games over .500, and St. Louis was a lowly four games under .500 in the regular season. The Celts were expected to breeze to their first NBA title. But the series ebbed and flowed, with the Hawks and Celtics each winning two games on the other team's court.

Hawks fans may disagree with that assessment, instead claiming the final Game 6 of the 1957–58 World Championship Series as the greatest ever. Another seesaw series began with the Hawks again winning Game 1 in Boston only to lose Game 4 on Kiel Auditorium's floor. The Hawks won Games 1 and 3, Boston won Games 2 and 4, but it was the pivotal Game 5 in Boston, a thrilling 102–100 St. Louis win, that provided the chance for the Hawks to win a world title at home in Game 6.

Game 6 is etched in St. Louis sports history and is on par with the St. Louis Cardinals' 1964 and 1982 seven-game World Series wins and the St. Louis Rams' Super Bowl win in 2000. Each of those events had an element that won the game

Bob Pettit blocks a lay-up attempt by Tommy Heinsohn during the 1958 Championship Series.

Bob Cousy finds his range at Kiel.

for the home team. The 1964 Game 7 had Cardinals Hall-of-Famer Bob Gibson's heroic nine-inning effort. The 1982 Game 7 had relief ace Bruce Sutter's ninth-inning strikeout of Milwaukee Brewer slugger Gorman Thomas. In 2000, Rams quarterback Kurt Warner completed a game-winning pass to Isaac Bruce.

On April 12, 1958, the St. Louis Hawks preceded them all by winning their one and only NBA Championship on the strength of Hall-of-Famer Bob Pettit's incredible 50-point performance. Big Blue poured in 19 of the team's final 21 points in the

110–109 victory before a delirious Kiel Auditorium standing-room-only crowd of 10,416. Pettit's mark still stands today as the NBA record for most points scored by an individual to win a championship.

Years later, members of that fabled Celtic team remember this loss by saying, "Bob Pettit's performance in Game 6 was Wilt Chamberlain, Elgin Baylor, and Michael Jordan all rolled up into one. Fantastic!"

The St. Louis–Boston rivalry was made great by the players who took the court for these legendary franchises. Over the years they played each other, the Hawks had eight Hall-of-Fame members and the Celtics had twelve. Remember these Boston legends: Bob Cousy, Bill Russell, Bill Sharman, Frank Ramsey, John Havlicek, Sam Jones, K. C. Jones, Tom Heinsohn, Arnie Risen, and Coach Red Auerbach. On the Hawks side, it was Bob Pettit, Cliff Hagan, Slater Martin, Lenny Wilkens, plus Coaches Alex Hannum and Red Holzman. The Celtics and Hawks share two Hall of Famers: Easy Ed Macauley and Clyde Lovellette.

Not a Hall of Famer but always a thorn in the Hawks' side, particularly to Bob Pettit, whom he often guarded, was "Jungle" Jim Loscutoff—a 6-5 bruiser whose No. 18 you kept an eye on all the time. Loscutoff tossed Pettit into the stands behind the basket in February of the 1956–57 season, breaking his wrist.

The Celtics–Hawks series always presented a new historical perspective. The night at Kiel before Game 3 of the 1956–57 series, Coach Auerbach challenged the height of the baskets on the court before tipoff, which escalated into a brief fist fight between Auerbach and Hawks owner Ben Kerner. Auerbach landed a punch to Kerner's face causing him to bleed, while the maintenance crew got their moment in the limelight as over 10,000 booing fans watched them confirm the regulation height of the basket.

There was the Hawks' bizarre attempt to tie the seventh game of the Championship Series in double overtime that same season. After Pettit sank two heart-stopping free throws at the end of regulation to tie the game, the "Old Rancher" Jack Coleman hit a jumper from the corner to tie the first overtime at the buzzer. Then came the wild decision by Coach Alex Hannum on how to try to tie the second overtime at the buzzer. With two seconds showing, he threw the ball the length of the court off the backboard into the waiting hands of Bob Pettit for a game-tying tip-in. Amazingly, Hannum did hit the board, but the Pettit tip-in rolled around and off the rim.

Alex Hannum

BOSTON CELTICS

FORWARD
TOMMY HEINSOHN

Ed Macauley rips a rebound away from Tom Heinsohn.

In Game 3 of the 1956–57 NBA Finals, the first basketball championship game played in St. Louis, the Boston Celtics' high-scoring, fiery forward Tom Heinsohn reacted to a call by screaming at the referees. He was given the first technical, and then continued the harassment, earning a second technical and automatic game ejection.

As "Tommy Gun" Heinsohn ran off the Kiel Auditorium floor to a thunder of boos, he gave the St. Louis crowd a parting gesture. That was enough for one young woman in the stands whose seat was on the aisle of the runway that Heinsohn had to pass on the way to the locker room. Continuing his gesture as he ran up the ramp, she could stand it no more and promptly leveled the Boston star with a solid whack across his head with her purse! Stunned and confused, the dazed Heinsohn gathered himself and jogged to the safety of the locker room.

Locked into memory are the titanic battles of Bill Russell, Charlie Share, and Bob Pettit fighting for rebounds with Russell or Pettit, or both, getting 25 to 30 rebounds in a game!

Another incredible matchup between the NBA's top two powerhouses was between point guards. Both in the Hall of Fame, Bob Cousy of the Celtics and Slater "Dugie" Martin of the Hawks went nose-to-nose, end-to-end for most of 48 minutes every time the teams met. Cousy, at 6-1, was a scoring machine able to hit twenty-foot set shots or drive the lane through traffic. He was also the wizard of deception handling the ball. The 5-10 veteran Martin was a scrappy, physical defender who wore out his opponents on defense and could score much the same way but not as often as the Cous.

Cousy has always said, "The only player in the league I didn't know if I could beat all the time or enjoy playing was Slater Martin. He could wear me out." With Martin, the feeling was mutual. Martin's ability to keep Cousy under 20 points per game more often than not gave St. Louis a chance to outdistance Boston.

Adding to the rivalry was the way the two teams had become intertwined between both players and management. Boston Coach Red Auerbach had been Hawks owner Ben Kerner's first coach of the Tri-City Hawks in the Basketball Association of America prior to the NBA's formation. The biggest trade in league history, which sent the rights to Bill Russell from St. Louis to Boston for Easy Ed Macauley and Cliff Hagan, also stirred the pot.

Macauley is at the center of so much of the Hawks–Celtics rivalry. He was the central player of the famous trade from the Hawks perspective, though the two-time All-American Hagan, who was a "throw-in" at the time, became a superstar performer for the champions. Macauley has the distinction of having played six seasons for Boston, becoming an all-pro for them with his jersey now hanging in the Boston Garden rafters. He was the Hawks' head coach against Boston in the 1959–60 Championship Series.

Few people know that Bob Cousy could have been a Hawk! He was the property of Kerner and Tri-Cities before being traded to Chicago and then on to Boston. Imagine a backcourt of Cousy and Martin on the Hawks, and what would that have meant to the history of the Celtics? How many titles wouldn't have been won in Beantown, and how many more in St. Louis? Fun questions to speculate.

Here are the player matchups that truly made the rivalry great: Russell vs. Share, Pettit vs. Heinsohn, Cousy vs. Martin, Hagan vs. Ramsey, and Jack McMahon vs. Bill Sharman. The 1959–60 teams added some new faces. Boston welcomed Hall-of-Fame guards Sam and K. C. Jones and baseball pitcher Gene Conley. While St. Louis's additions were guards Si Green and Johnny McCarthy, both from the Cincinnati Royals in exchange for fan favorite and Missouri native Win Wilfong, plus future Hall-of-Fame center and high-scoring Clyde Lovellette. Al Ferrari, a solid player at guard during the first St. Louis seasons, came back and played well after finishing military service.

Charlie Share splits defenders for two points.

Voice of the Hawks Buddy Blattner sits in his perch high above the court at Kiel Auditorium next to his between-periods host Jim Butler of KMOX Radio at a home game.

The last chance at beating the Celtics came in the 1960–61 campaign when the two again met in the NBA Finals. Now future Hall-of-Famer Lenny Wilkens was added to the Hawks' high-scoring machine. However, an excruciating seven-game semifinal series against the coming power in the West, Jerry West, Elgin Baylor, and the Los Angeles Lakers, forced the Hawks to expend a lot of energy. St. Louis won a narrow two-point last-second victory in Game 7. Then Boston got up 2–0 in the Finals and never looked back, winning the series in five games.

The memories of the Hawks and Celtics in the 1950s and early 1960s are priceless. They were the franchises that alerted the nation to this exciting new national professional league and brought national television in the form of NBC Sports to the table for a national broadcast in the middle of that first confrontation, Game 3 in 1956.

Whenever the Celtics came to Kiel to play the Hawks, there would be a buzz around the city that day. Businessmen scurried around for tickets, and fans who couldn't get in the sold-out auditorium scheduled their evening around listening to the play-by-play of Buddy Blattner on KMOX Radio. A St. Louis–Boston NBA game was like Cards–Cubs in baseball. They indeed were "those hated Celtics."

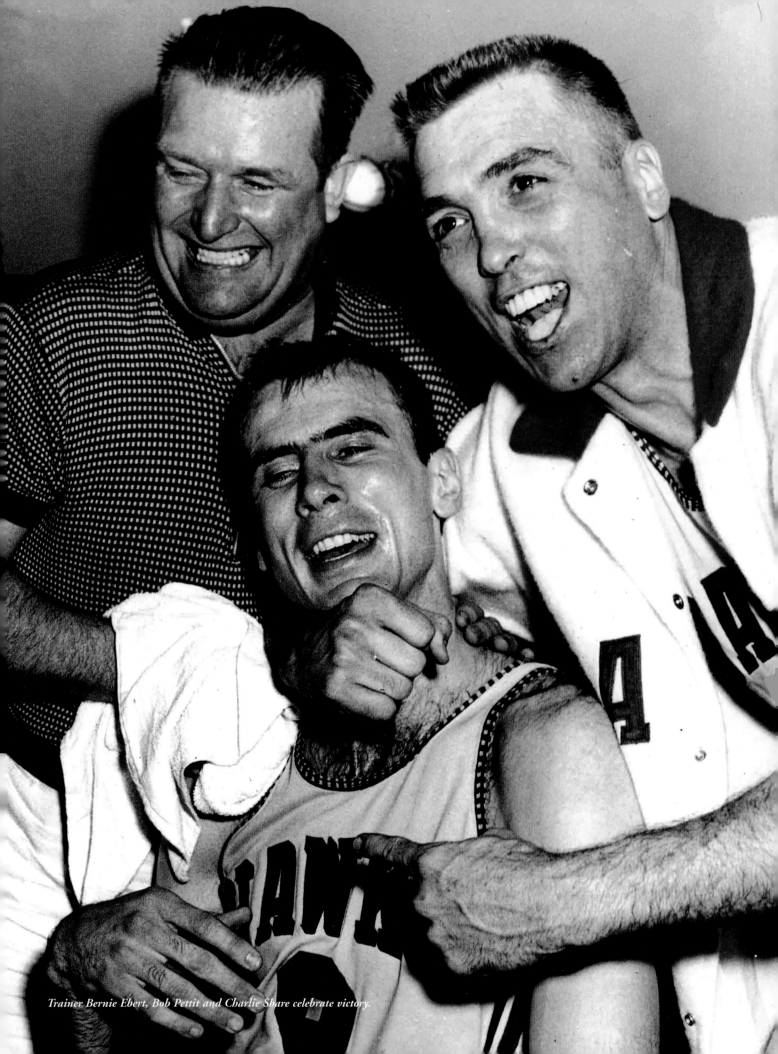

Trainer Bernie Ebert, Bob Pettit and Charlie Share celebrate victory.

4 THE WORLD CHAMPION ST. LOUIS HAWKS

"We couldn't go back to Boston and expect to win again," said the late Med Park, the gritty guard off the bench for the 1957–58 St. Louis Hawks. He was remembering how the team felt as they came together in the pregame locker room of Game 6 of the World Championship Series against the defending champion Celtics.

It was dawn on April 12, 1958, as St. Louisans woke up to their morning *St. Louis Globe-Democrat* hungry for the scene-setting stories in the sports section to get them ready to descend on downtown and Kiel Auditorium. They were ready to give their beloved Hawks all the support they would need to dethrone the champs. Up three games to two in the best-of-seven Championship Series, St. Louis could create history that night.

Just the day before at a Concordia Seminary practice, Hawks Coach Alex Hannum chose not to rile up his opponents. Instead, he praised them to the local and national media. With all due diplomacy, Hannum said, "Bill Sharman and Bob Cousy were voted the top guard combination in the NBA, and you can also say Frank Ramsey is the best sixth man in the league. Bill Russell was voted NBA MVP and Tom Heinsohn is an All-Star team performer. That's an awfully strong line-up. I just hope we play hard again."

Nervous excitement was everywhere in the city, which for this one day had forgotten there was a baseball season underway. After a long day of waiting, the ball was tipped in the air at 8:30 p.m. with Jim Crews at the mike until the great Buddy Blattner arrived from his baseball game of the week telecast. Game 6 aired on KWK, with color man Jim Butler and a national television audience. Like a World Series game, every bounce of the ball meant so much, and it would be a roller-coaster day for the fans.

The first half of the opening period belonged to the desperate Celtics, but ironically when the limping Bill Russell entered the game at the six-minute mark, the Hawks took over. The Hawks were tentative, cold, and tight at the start, trailing 7–4 early. Russell was playing with torn tendons in his ankle. He couldn't cut sharply or jump aggressively, which played into the hands of "Big Blue" Bob Pettit.

Pettit was all over the court. He drove for the basket, found openings for his patented jump shot, and was around the basket for second-chance points. In all, he scored 12 of the Hawks' 22 points in the first quarter for a 22–18 lead.

The seesaw struggle began in earnest as the Celtics hung tough, twice grabbing one-point leads in the second stanza. But the Hawks went on runs, building the lead to as many as eight and settling for the 57–52 halftime edge. Pettit added 9 more for 21 points, plus the Hawks got 8 apiece from the red-hot Cliff Hagan, who'd had a sensational series averaging 25 points per game. Jack Coleman, the "Old Rancher," also had 8.

The Hawks came out of the halftime dressing room ready to put this one away, but even after some quick baskets and a ten-point lead, they couldn't shake the Celts. St. Louis's fiery leader,

Cliff Hagan draws the attention of the Celtic defenders.

Slater Martin, had done a remarkable job all series long on Hall-of-Fame guard Bob Cousy. The Cous had only two points at the half, but he held the Celtics close in the third quarter. He scored seven points and had several key assists as Boston stayed within six, 83–77. Pettit added 10 more points for a total of 31 after three periods.

Out came the teams for the fourth quarter, and Blattner announced, "This is what we've been playing for, and the Hawks have just 12 minutes to go to win their first NBA title. Let's go win it."

In the forefront of Hawks' fans' minds were the many great fourth quarters they had witnessed the

last couple of seasons from Boston. The Celts would come at them with a fury. Boston was getting a tremendous game from Russell's substitute, center Lou Tsioropoulos, pronounced "Siropolous," who ended up with 14 points to go along with another center, Arnie Risen, who added 12.

A hush fell across Kiel as the Celtics exploded on a 9–1 run and took the fourth quarter lead 86–84. First, a Martin free throw made it 86–85. But the Celts bounced right back and scored for an 88–85 lead. The crowd roared again as Jack McMahon hit a 25-foot set shot, Ed Macauley made a pair of free throws, and Pettit took an amazing feed from Charlie Share for a layup and a three-point lead.

Pettit is out-rebounded by Cousy and Macauley, as Russell and Ramsey look on.

Frank Ramsey shoots a free throw in Game 4 of the 1961–62 NBA Championship Series (Clyde Lovellette on the right).

Once again, Boston answered behind a free throw by Ramsey and a set shot by Sharman to tie the score at 91.

The rugged tone of play forced Blattner to say, "Folks, things are getting pretty rough out on the court now as we head down the stretch." The play was fierce. After the reliable captain Share blocked a big shot with 8:10 to play, the behemoths Russell and Share started pushing and shoving each other and had to be separated. Then Bill Sharman got into a jawing match with the Hawks. Referee Mendy Rudolph calmed everyone down and play went on.

Pettit had made two points early in the period for a tally of 33, but he was about to make basketball history. Telling the coach and players to "just get me the ball" in an unusual demonstrative show on the sidelines, Pettit made good on his word. He had rested for the first three minutes of the period but came back at the urging of the crowd with the Hawks behind and nine minutes to play.

With the clock running down and the team in a tight battle, it became apparent that the voice of the Hawks only needed to know one name on the offensive end of the game. "Pettit has it, he shoots, he scores! . . . Pettit drives for the basket, he goes up, and in! . . . Pettit with the rebound, he puts it up, it's GO-O-O-O-D!!!"

With 2:20 to go, the Hawks had a five-point lead, 105–100. But Cousy and Sharman wouldn't quit. It was 105–104 after four points from Cousy and 1:45 still left. There was an exchange of free throws, and then Pettit got loose for a layup and a 108–107 edge.

Each team got a chance to score, and both missed. The last miss coming off the rim from a short 10-foot Cousy shot for the lead. So who got the most important rebound in Hawks history with a one-point lead with 26 seconds left? Back-up rookie guard Win Wilfong, of course, who grabbed the carom and got the ball to Pettit, who scored points 49 and 50.

With over 10,600 fans standing and holding their breath, the Hawks let Sharman go the length of the court for a layup to close to 110–109, and now with 12 seconds and no timeouts, Coleman passed it in to Martin who dribbled around without getting fouled, passing to Easy Ed Macauley with four seconds remaining. As time expired, the horn sounded and Macauley launched the basketball with both hands 50 feet into the air as hoards rushed the court! **THE HAWKS ARE THE CHAMPIONS OF THE WORLD! THE HAWKS ARE THE CHAMPIONS OF THE WORLD!**

The fans were delirious inside Kiel, and horns were honking around the city. Even the usual cool, calm Blattner had lost it on the air, screaming numerous times, "The Hawks are World Champions! It feels so doggone good!"

Pettit had turned in the greatest performance in NBA history to that time, scoring 50 points, a feat that has never been eclipsed by another NBA player in a championship-determining game. Hagan was next with 15, and Macauley, who in the fourth quarter had four assists and a few key rebounds still, loves to needle when fans reminisce about this greatest night in St. Louis basketball history and Pettit's incomparable performance– "But without my two free throws, my only two points in the game, we lose, don't we!?"

In the *Wall Street Journal* on April 13, 1958, the first line of the story read, "St. Louis is the basketball capital of the world today."

Bill Sharman shoots a free throw at Kiel during the 1961–62 NBA Championship Series.

5 THE CHAMPIONSHIP TEAMS

Four times in 13 seasons, Hawks fans got to revel in the action of a championship series. These teams battled their way through the Western Division regular-season and postseason competition to engage the mighty Boston Celtics. Were it not for the greatest franchise in NBA history standing in the way of the highly skilled Hawks, more championships quite probably would have flowed through St. Louis.

What's for sure in NBA lore is that these series, in particular the first two, brought the NBA to the forefront of sports fans nationally and earned a spot for the sport on national television. The allure was the intensity and closeness of the games, the great drama that unfolded, and the magnitude of the stars, Pettit, Hagan, and Martin vs. Russell, Cousy, and Heinsohn. Boston vs. St. Louis was the pinnacle of pro basketball.

The Finalist
1956–1957 Western Division Champions
Record: 34–38
Won a three-way playoff against
Ft. Wayne and Minneapolis
Won NBA Semifinals over Minneapolis 3–0
Lost in NBA Finals to Boston 4–3

Buoyed by their unexpected playoff appearance in their first season, the Hawks were anxious to pick up where they left off. Solid guard Al Ferrari was off to the military and only veteran forward Jack Coleman was on the team to help deflect some attention from the NBA's Most Valuable Player, Bob Pettit. The brain trust of Ben Kerner and Marty Blake needed to deal for a point-producing forward and a floor leader at guard.

The Hawks had the No. 2 draft choice, and they used it to complete one of the most important trades in NBA history. Knowing University of San Francisco superstar 6-11 center Bill Russell had no interest in being drafted by Rochester, who had the No. 1 pick, nor the Hawks at No. 2, the Hawks were able to grab his rights after Rochester took Duquesne guard Si Green. The Hawks then traded Russell to Boston for veteran all-pro and St. Louisan Ed Macauley and a rookie two-time All-American from Kentucky named Cliff Hagan.

The likes of Pettit surrounded by his protector center Charlie Share, Coleman, and Macauley with guards Jack McMahon and Med Park, St. Louis was close to contending. However, they still needed that all-pro guard to match-up with Boston's brilliant court general Bob Cousy. The savvy Kerner found a way to outfox his division opponents and entice four-time NBA champion and future Hall-of-Fame guard Slater Martin to allow a trade with New York for a promising previous No. 1 draft pick Willie Naulls.

Martin stabilized the offensive attack and became Cousy's biggest nemesis. There was still one key component missing from the puzzle: The right coach to lead the team. Kerner fired Coach Red Holzman, who had a 14–19 record, in January, and replaced him with Martin. Martin, however, only lasted five games with the player-coach tag, and he encouraged Kerner to give the job to another player, the fiery Alex Hannum.

Hannum took the Hawks to the title by going 20–19 the rest of the way. He then led them to a three-way playoff win for the division title, beating the Minneapolis Lakers and then beating them again in a three-game sweep for the right to play the Eastern Division winner, the Boston Celtics, in their first NBA Finals.

6
Western Division Titles

4
ConferenceTitles

4
NBA Finals

1
NBA Championship

The St. Louis Hawks playing the San Francisco Warriors at Kiel Auditorium.

Pettit attempts blocking a shot against the Detroit Pistons.

Who would have guessed a key to the season's success would develop from a Bob Pettit injury. A February 15 broken-wrist injury took Pettit out for a few games and allowed the youngster, Cliff Hagan, to finally get some playing time as a starter at forward. He was immediately a point producer, so when Pettit returned, Coach Hannum sent Macauley to the bench, backing up both Pettit and Hagan. The Hawks now had a tremendous additional scoring punch. Hagan averaged over 20 points per game throughout the playoffs.

The Hawks shocked the league by beating the Celtics in their own backyard in Game 1 of the Finals. The Hawks went toe-to-toe with the heavily favored Bostonians all the way to the last shot of a double-overtime seventh game, losing 125–123.

1957–1958 Western Division Champions
RECORD: 41–31
WON NBA SEMIFINALS OVER MINNEAPOLIS 4–3
WON NBA WORLD CHAMPIONSHIP
OVER BOSTON 4–2

The fans were ready, the players were ready, and by mid-December the Hawks had found their stride. The team had balance on both ends of the court with the regular starting five of Share, Pettit, and Hagan up front and McMahon and Martin in the backcourt. Adding great depth off the bench were Macauley, Jack Coleman, rookie Win Wilfong, and Mizzou's Med Park, all contributing points and defense as the club built momentum.

St. Louis won the division by eight games, but their opponent in the semifinals, Detroit, had beaten them five of the last six meetings. However, Hagan, who scored 38, 27, 28, and finally 32 points in the series-clinching fifth game, led the Hawks and earned Cliff a long standing ovation at the end of Game 5. Hagan had become a league superstar alongside Pettit, who also kept his scoring around 20 points per game.

WIN WILFONG

WORLD CHAMPIONS
1958

Official Magazine 35¢

ST. LOUIS HAWKS

Clyde Lovellette challenges Bill Russell's shot.

As the Finals began for the second straight year in Boston, the Hawks served notice by having the poise to win a thrilling 104–102 Game 1. The magnificent Hagan dropped in a game-high 33 points, and the All-Pro Pettit was right behind him with 30 points. Game 2 was a Celtic blowout made memorable by the first-ever network telecast of an NBA game by NBC Television, which paid Boston $15,000 for the TV rights.

Game 3 was St. Louis's chance to shine as a city, packing Kiel with over 10,000 rabid fans and a nearby Opera House full of fans watching on closed-circuit TV. Superstar center Bill Russell was injured in the game and would miss all but the final game of the series. Without Big Bill clogging the middle and blocking shots, the likes of Pettit and Hagan moved more freely around the lane, and Game 4 was a 109–96 blowout for the Hawks.

Celtic star Bob Cousy did all he could to keep Boston in it by grabbing 13 rebounds to go with 10 assists and 24 points, a typical Cousy night.

Game 5 was a classic come-from-behind effort for St. Louis. They trailed by 15 points in the contest before rallying in the fourth quarter. Demonic efforts from Pettit, Macauley, Share, and Coleman on the boards, plus Martin's heroic effort holding Cousy to just 10 points, led to an exhausting 102–100 win in the Boston Garden. Pettit scored 33 points in the process and Hagan another 21.

Russell returned to the lineup, though gimpy, for the Game 6 elimination game for Boston. Back at Kiel, the Hawks were riveted on winning at home. The Celtics held in gamely in the first half, holding the lead on several occasions. Finally, by the half St. Louis had a five-point edge, 57–52, carried by

JUST THE TICKET!

L.A. Laker Elgin Baylor waits on a pass as Lenny Wilkens (32) attempts to get back on defense, with Hawks forward Mike Farmer (12).

Hawks owner Ben Kerner is presented with a special award from the St. Louis Chamber of Commerce by KMOX Radio Vice President and General Manager Robert F. Hyland (middle) while Hawks General Manager Marty Blake (left) looks on.

Pettit's 21 points. Who knew they were about to witness history for Pettit and the team?

Pettit took over the game with the Hawks up by two, 89–87, and less than six minutes left to play. After a memorable time out in which Big Blue asked his teammates to feed him, Pettit ripped off 19 of the last 21 points for an NBA-record 50 points in the final game. The champagne began to flow in metro St. Louis, the basketball capital of the world.

1959–60 Western Division Champions
Record: 46–29
Won NBA Semifinals over Detroit 4–1
Lost in NBA Finals to Boston 4–3

After winning the championship in 1958, the continuity was disrupted by a poor decision by owner Ben Kerner to let Coach Alex Hannum go into a contract dispute. His replacement, Andy Phillip, lasted just 10 games, and Kerner replaced him with St. Louis favorite Easy

Ed Macauley. Still a player at the time, Macauley made the decision to move to the bench, and he led the club to a tremendous regular-season finish and all-time Hawk best at 49–23.

But this great team, which outdistanced the Minneapolis Lakers by a whopping 16 games, had a hiccup at the wrong time, and they were upset in six games by the Los Angeles Lakers in the division championship series.

However, St. Louis bounced back under the 31-year-old Coach Macauley and again won big, with a 46–29 regular-season record. Gone were Slater Martin, Jack McMahon, and Charlie Share, being replaced by the likes of Johnny McCarthy and Si Green at guard and Hall-of-Fame center Clyde Lovellette at center. This time, after falling behind the Lakers three games to two in the division finals as they did the year before, the Hawks bounced back, winning Games 6 and 7 to earn a third trip to

Lenny Wilkens goes up strong against Los Angeles Lakers standout Elgin Baylor.

meet the Boston club in the NBA Finals. It was the unexpected 16 points and 13 assists from Si Green that carried the Hawks to a 96–87 win over the Lakers in a nerve-wracking affair.

In Games 1, 3, and 5 of the NBA Finals, the Celtics annihilated St. Louis by 18, 16, and 25 points respectively. But the scrappy Hawks took the beatings and won Games 2, 4, and 6 to set up a third Game 7 in the history of these two rivals.

The Hawks were major underdogs in Game 7 at Boston Garden with some 13,909 Hawks-haters rattling the rafters, but the Hawks kept coming. After one period, the visitors led by a point, 30–29, but a 41-point barrage by Cousy, Russell,

Heinsohn, and friends buried the Birds. Nineteen points and 14 assists by the magician, Cousy, 24 from Frank Ramsey, and 22 from both Russell and Heinsohn carried the day and the title to Boston, 122–103.

1960–1961 Western Division Champions
RECORD: 51–28
WON THE DIVISION TITLE OVER LOS ANGELES 4–3
LOST THE NBA FINALS TO BOSTON 4–1

Despite another bizarre coaching change that replaced Macauley with Paul Seymour, the results remained the same. A new franchise record was set at 51–28, and the team was on pace to get back to the finals for a fourth time in five seasons.

New Head Coach Ed Macauley is the youngest in the NBA at 33.

The cast members changed little with Pettit, Hagan, and Lovellette still intact on the frontline, while McCarthy, Ferrari, and Green made up a solid backcourt. The new and welcome addition was the brilliant rookie from Providence College, Lenny Wilkens. Soon, he was feeding Big Blue, and nobody appreciated his passing and ball-handling skills more than Pettit. It didn't take a genius to figure out that getting the ball to Pettit and Hagan would put points on the board, and yet Wilkens still scored 890 points as a rookie.

Getting to the Finals again proved to be a challenge, even though the Hawks won the West by a whopping 15 games over Los Angeles. The Lakers, led by stars Elgin Baylor, Jerry West, and "Hot Rod" Hundley, proved to be a handful. They extended the series to seven games. The pivotal

Game 4 featured the Hawks down two games to one. Rookie sensation Lenny Wilkens grabbed a rebound and was fouled with six seconds left and L.A. up by a point. With the Los Angeles crowd hooting and hollering, the rookie calmly made both shots to win the game, 114–113. St. Louis won Game 7 in a 105–103 breathtaker at Keil Auditorium.

The rested Celtics, now with Sam and K. C. Jones adding to the misery of the opponents, blasted the mentally and physically tired Hawks, 129–95, in Game 1. The series went only five games, as the Hawks were blown out three times. The clincher was a 121–112 loss at the Boston Garden, giving the Celtics their third-straight NBA title and fourth in five seasons. It was the last visit to the NBA Finals for the St. Louis Hawks.

BOB
PETTIT

ST. LOUIS
Hawks

6 Basketball Hall of Fame: St. Louis Hawks Legends

St. Louis has been a city graced by the presence of many sports legends. They began early with the four-time baseball champion St. Louis Browns teams of 1885–1888. Tennis star Arthur Ashe, the bowling Budweiser team, track Olympian Jackie Joyner-Kersee, and golf Hall-of-Famer Hale Irwin all made their mark. With the addition of all those St. Louis Cardinals, a pair of St. Louis Blues, and four National Football League Hall-of-Famers from the Football Cardinals, "Hall of Fame" is, indeed, a common phrase in the Gateway City.

However, nothing is common or ordinary about producing no less than eight NBA Hall-of-Famers wearing the red and white of the Hawks in just thirteen seasons. It takes Hall-of-Fame–caliber players and coaches to consistently win division, conference, and league titles, and St. Louis had more than their share of it all.

Bob Pettit and Elgin Baylor diving for an errant ball.

CLIFF HAGAN

FORWARD, NUMBER 16
6-4 210 LBS.
UNIVERSITY OF KENTUCKY
YEARS WITH THE HAWKS: 10 SEASONS, 1956–1966
ACQUIRED IN TRADE FROM BOSTON IN 1955

Cliff Hagan, dubbed "Little Abner" by broadcaster Bud Blattner, was a fan favorite for 10 seasons. He came to the Hawks from the Boston Celtics in a trade that brought him and Ed Macauley to St. Louis for the rights to Bill Russell. Hawks Coach Red Holzman projected Hagan as a guard, but after an injury to superstar Bob Pettit, Cliff came off the bench as a forward, leading to a prolific scoring and rebounding career.

His lifetime scoring average in St. Louis was 18 points per game in the regular season, but the average pumped up to 20 points per game in the playoffs. Hagan was "money" for the Hawks in big games. He could pass the ball to fellow star Bob Pettit as well, and they made an unstoppable duo. In the championship season, Hagan entered the NBA's "Select Circle" of scorers by putting up 40 points on three different occasions and 41 on one.

He starred in that championship playoff run, shooting a scintillating 50 percent from the field and averaging 27.7 points per game to lead the team. He appeared in five NBA All-Star games and twice was named Second Team All-Pro.

He was known for his patented hook shots from almost anywhere in the front court with either hand. Hagan would fade away with his hook so it would be completely out of reach from taller opponents. He added reverse layups on his drives to the basket to get past the opposition. He was inducted into the Hall of Fame in 1977.

CLYDE LOVELLETTE

ST. LOUIS HAWKS

CLYDE LOVELLETTE
SWEEPS BY AN OPPONENT

CENTER, NUMBER 34
6-10 235 LBS.
KANSAS UNIVERSITY
YEARS WITH THE HAWKS: 4 SEASONS, 1958–1962
ACQUIRED BY TRADE FROM CINCINNATI IN 1958

Clyde Lovellette, dubbed "Boom Boom" by Bud Blattner, won a World Championship at Minneapolis in the 1953–54 season as backup center to NBA great George Mikan. Over the next three seasons, he starred as the team's center, averaging 18, 20, and 21 points per game. After one season in Cincinnati, Hawks owner Ben Kerner showedClyde his worth by trading five players to get the smooth-shooting center.

He joined the front line of Bob Pettit and Cliff Hagan for the season following the Hawks' World Championship. Together, they formed the best front line in the NBA, averaging over 70 points per game. Kerner called them "the Unmatchables." Lovellette was a tremendous shooter facing the basket 10 to 20 feet outside, forcing the opposing center to come out of the lane to guard him. He averaged 14, 20, 22, and 20 points per game in his four St. Louis seasons on the way to the Basketball Hall of Fame.

His jumping ability and stamina were questions when he arrived, but Hawks Coach Ed Macauley had the cure. Ankle weights, orange juice with raw eggs in it, and long workout sessions dramatically improved Clyde's defensive skills. He became one of the league's best, according to other coaches, against the unstoppable Wilt Chamberlain and Bill Russell.

Clyde played on Kansas's NCAA Championship team in 1952. Ironically, his best collegiate game came against Saint Louis University, when he scored 44 points in a win. As a Hawk, his best scoring totals were 39 points on two occasions: January 24, 1960, against New York and January 31, 1961, against Syracuse.

While the Hawks didn't win the championship with Lovellette, he was irreplaceable on their potent front line and played in two championship series against the Boston Celtics. His Hall of Fame induction was in 1988.

"EASY" ED MACAULEY

FORWARD, NUMBER 20
6-8 190 LBS.
SAINT LOUIS UNIVERSITY
YEARS WITH THE HAWKS: 5 SEASONS, 1956–1959
(PLAYER), 1959–1961 (COACH)
ACQUIRED BY TRADE FROM BOSTON IN 1955

The greatest basketball player born and raised in St. Louis without question is Ed Macauley. He was a two-time All-America player for his Saint Louis University teams, which in the 1947–48 season won the national collegiate basketball championship. He went on to stardom in the NBA, first with the Boston Celtics as a three-time All-NBA First Team member, then to the Hawks as a vital piece of the 1958 championship team, and finally as the successful head coach of the NBA Finalist Hawks in 1960.

ED MACAULEY
ST. LOUIS
Hawks

Ed was a silky-smooth shooter, the first Celtic to average 20 points per game, and the only Celtic whose number is retired and hanging in the Boston Garden without having won an NBA title with Boston. He became a Hawk in what is still called the most important trade in NBA history, bringing Hall- of-Fame center Bill Russell to Boston via the Hawks' first-round draft pick in 1955 for two Hall of Famers, Macauley and the great Cliff Hagan.

That trade turned both St. Louis and Boston into championship teams and created a rivalry that many claim as the most important factor in the evolution of the NBA into a nationally known league. Macauley gave the Hawks needed veteran leadership and a scoring punch to take some of the pressure and tension off the remarkable superstar Bob Pettit. He averaged 16 and 14 points per game in his two St. Louis seasons while rotating at the forward position with Pettit and Hagan.

The season the Hawks won the NBA championship, 1958–59, Macauley was asked to become the head coach after just 10 games, and he retired as a player. He showed his skill as a leader of men in two seasons, winning 89 games while posting a .650 winning percentage, which stands today as the best winning percentage by any Hawks coach, St. Louis or Atlanta, in history. His teams won two Western Division titles, and in 1959–60, his Hawks nearly upset the heavily favored Celtics, losing in the seventh game of the NBA Finals.

Easy Ed Macauley, as he is lovingly called in his native St. Louis, was elected as the youngest player ever to enter the Basketball Hall of Fame at age 32 in 1960.

SLATER "DUGIE" MARTIN

GUARD, NUMBER 22
5-10 170 LBS.
UNIVERSITY OF TEXAS
YEARS WITH THE HAWKS: 4 SEASONS, 1956–1960
ACQUIRED BY TRADE FROM
NEW YORK IN DECEMBER 1956

Slater Martin said that he was "retiring" when the Minneapolis Lakers honored his salary demands after he was the playmaker for their four NBA championship teams, 1950, 1952, 1953, and 1954. But Ben Kerner's Hawks had all the elements of a

champion except a point guard to bring the ball up the court and feed his high-scoring front line. He cleverly arranged for the New York Knicks, to acquire the rights to Martin from the Hawks chief rival Minneapolis, and then he swung a deal to get Martin.

The Hawks now had their man to defend Boston's incredible high-scoring guard Bob Cousy. A seven-time NBA All-Star in an 11-year career, Martin was hailed by Cousy as "his toughest rival in the NBA and the one guy I'm not sure I can beat on a given night." Martin averaged nearly 10 points and 4 assists per game while holding down the opposition's top guard below his season averages.

Martin was fiercely competitive and could always get a rise out of the rabid St. Louis fans. He would steal a pass, race down the court, and selflessly look for the dish to a trailing Hagan or Pettit for the layin. Dugie would set up the offense and be the first back on defense.

When Martin was slipped out of Minneapolis to New York and then to St. Louis, the Hawks were struggling several games under .500.

While they played the rest of the 1956–57 season a little under .500, they jelled as a unit with Martin leading the way. They took Boston to seven tough games in the Finals, and the following season, they won the championship. It was Slater Martin who took the inbound pass with seconds to play and dribbled around, finally passing to Ed Macauley as the clock struck zero at Kiel Auditorium. St. Louis went delirious with their first and only championship. Slater was inducted with five World Championship rings into the Basketball Hall of Fame in 1981.

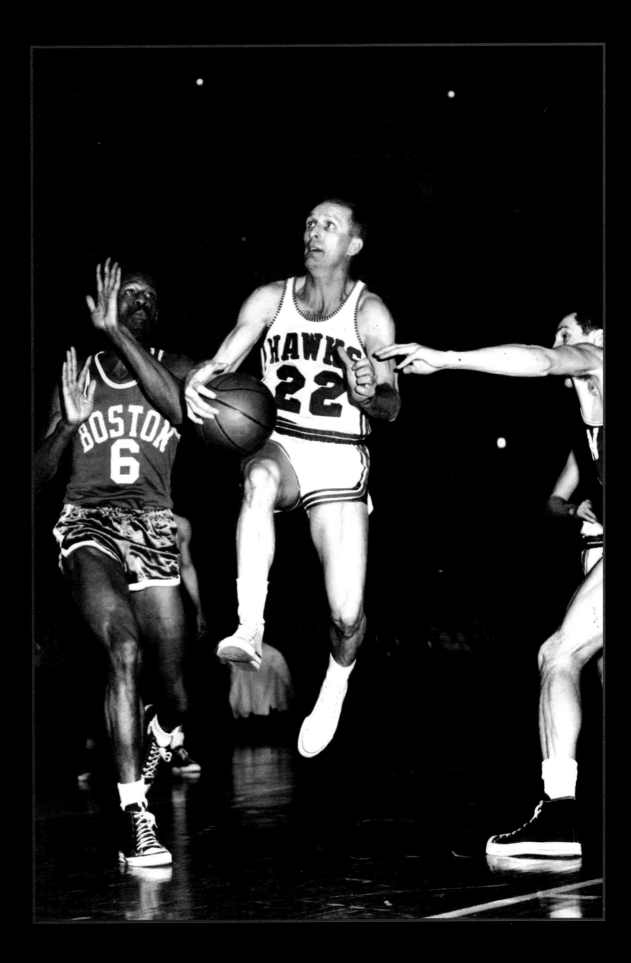

BOB PETTIT

ST. LOUIS HAWKS

BOB PETTIT
GOES UP FOR A SHOT

FORWARD, NUMBER 9
6-9 215 LBS.
LOUISIANA STATE UNIVERSITY
YEARS WITH THE HAWKS: 11 SEASONS—(ONE IN
MILWAUKEE), 1954–1965
DRAFTED NO. 1 IN THE 1954 NBA DRAFT

The greatest player in Hawks' history and selected as one of the 50 greatest in NBA history in a vote of an elite group of 50 basketball experts, Bob Pettit was a Milwaukee Hawk as the NBA's 1954 Rookie of the Year. He averaged 20.4 points, 13.8 rebounds, and 3 assists for the NBA's worst team.

Once in St. Louis, Pettit became a home town hero in a league with only Stan "The Man" Musial of the St. Louis Cardinals. Jump shots, hook shots, driving layups, and the best in the game at picking up second-chance points off his shots, "Big Blue," as nicknamed by Blattner, earned a phenomenal 10 straight selections to the All-NBA First Team, earned 2 Most Valuable Player Awards, won 2 NBA scoring titles, and 1 rebounding title, was the first player in history to score 20,000 career points, played in 11 All-Star games, and was the All-Star MVP a record four times, a record which stands today.

Nothing says more of true greatness than when it is spoken by your teammates and opponents. His greatness extended off the court as well, where Pettit was a humble, quiet man who cherished his time with teammates, friends, and especially his family.

Pettit's fabulous career totals include: 11 seasons, 891 games played, 23,344 total points in regular-season, postseason, and All-Star games, 12,849 regular-season rebounds, plus 1,304 in playoffs and 178 in All-Star games. He averaged 26.4 points and 16.2 rebounds. From 1955 to 1960, Bob held almost every NBA single-season record offensively and in rebounds.

Big Blue was his best against the best. He came up strong in big games. Against the long-recognized best defender in NBA history, Boston's 11-time NBA champion Bill Russell, Pettit gave him the most concern. Many of his best games were against Russell, where he frequently exceeded 30 points per game. "Bob made the words 'second effort' a permanent part of this sport's vocabulary," Russell said with admiration.

"Bob kept coming at you more than any man I ever played against in the game of basketball. By the third quarter of those Hawks games I'd beholding the bottom of my shorts asking Red (Auerbach), 'Isn't there anyone else who can try to stop this guy?'"

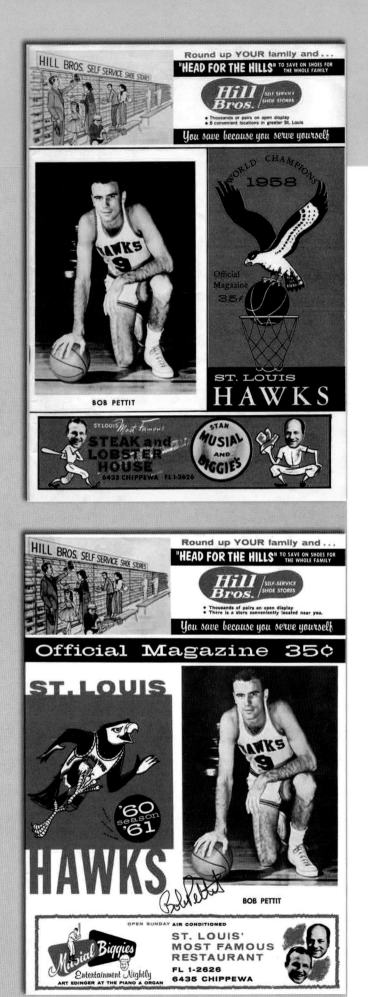

Without doubt, Pettit's top achievement in pro basketball still stands as a record today. On April 12, 1958, in the pivotal Game 6 of the NBA Finals with the Hawks leading the series three games to two, the Hawks were in the fourth quarter at the historic Kiel Auditorium, barely ahead of the explosive Celtics, 89–87, with six minutes on the clock. It was then when the reserved superstar made his presence known in the time out huddle and asked for the ball.

He got it the rest of the way, scoring an astonishing 19 of 21 points for St. Louis, carrying them on his back to a dramatic one-point World Championship victory, 110–109. His 50 points stand today as the most ever scored by an individual to win the NBA championship.

Pettit, who once scored 57 points in a game and twice had 35 rebounds in one game, was inducted into the Basketball Hall of Fame in 1970. By the way, as a high schooler, Bob was cut from the basketball team as a freshman and sophomore before averaging 27 points per game as a junior.

LENNY WILKENS

GUARD, NUMBER 14
6-1 185 LBS.
PROVIDENCE COLLEGE
YEARS WITH THE HAWKS: 8 SEASONS, 1960–1968
DRAFTED NO. 1 BY THE HAWKS IN 1960

It was Len Wilkens' destiny to become a St. Louis Hawk. After all, he owed the fans of the city something good. It was his Providence College Friars who had just ended the hopes of a second National Invitational Tournament championship for Saint Louis University, beating SLU in the 1960 Finals. New Hawks Coach Paul Seymour and General Manager Marty Blake both wanted to draft Wilkens, but owner Ben Kerner was unimpressed.

He didn't have imposing stature, he wasn't a loud, fiery guy on the floor, and he wasn't a speed merchant, but Wilkens had an intelligent approach to the game. He outwitted his opponents and beat them with his quickness and silky style. Once inserted into the lineup after a quality performance against the Knicks, scoring 14 points playing much of the game for the first time, he became a starter. Kerner was impressed, and he bellowed out behind a big, fat cigar while standing on the Madison Square Garden court post game, "I wouldn't trade Lenny Wilkens for $50,000 and the whole Knicks team!"

Wilkens could shoot the set shot or slither through the lane keeping the ball out of reach with a swooping left-handed layup. Lenny always went to his left and everybody in the arena knew it, but they couldn't stop it. The Hawks won 51 games and went to the finals only to lose to Boston in his rookie year.

He learned much that first season, and had one of his career-best moments. In Game 4 of the Western Conference Finals against Los Angelesdown two games to one playing in L.A., Wilkenswas fouled with no time left and St. Louis down one. He calmly made two free throws against the roaring crowd to win the game, and the Hawks went on to win the series.

He survived three coaching changes in St. Louis: Paul Seymour who drafted him, Harry Gallatin, and finally Richie Guerin. Averaging 12 to 18 points per game, his best two seasons were the last ones. He averaged 20 points and 8 assists in 1966–67 and 22 points and 8 assists in 1967–68. He was runner-up for the NBA Most Valuable Player Award in 1968.

His playing career went seven more seasons, four in Seattle, two in Cleveland, and one in Portland, never getting to taste the championship as a player. He was a nine-time All-Star averaging more than eight assists per game for six straight seasons.

He won the NBA championship as a coach, leading Seattle to the 1978–79 World Title. He was NBA Coach of the Year for the Hawks in 1993–94. Overall, Wilkens coached 29 seasons in a remarkable NBA career.

Wilkens is one of two men in basketball history to be inducted twice into the Basketball Hall of Fame. He entered the Shrine as a player in 1989 and again as a coach in 1998. He has coached more NBA games than any man in history, 2,406, and has more wins, 1,292, than any coach in history. He is most proud of coaching the United States Olympic Team to the basketball Gold Medal in 1996.

COACH ALEX HANNUM

Years with the Hawks: 2 seasons, 1956–1957 (player-coach), 1957–1958 (coach)

Alex Hannum didn't apply for the coaching job, he got it by default. He was an average player in the right place at the right time when Ben Kerner decided to again change coaches when interim player-coach Slater Martin said after a few games in the 1956–57 season that he couldn't do both jobs and lead the Hawks on the floor. Martin suggested the fiery veteran player, Hannum, and Kerner grudgingly consented.

Kerner frankly didn't like much about Hannum, his penchant for drinking, late-night partying, and speaking his mind, but he would like his coaching. It was a pivotal moment in St. Louis Hawks' history. His strategy was easy to follow. Pass the ball, move the ball to the open man, play hard defense, and above all, get the ball to Bob Pettit.

In the 1956–57 season, Hannum guided the Hawks from last place in the Western Division at 19–23 in late January, to the seventh game of the NBA Finals and a double-overtime loss to the Boston Celtics by just two points! The team melded as friends and teammates under the man who inherited this Buddy Blattner nickname, "The Old Sarge."

Hannum's troops fought through a broken wrist for Pettit and saw Ed Macauley pick up the missing points, putting up 16 to 25 points per game in Big Blue's absence. Hannum's wisdom wrenched Cliff Hagan off the bench where the previous coach had him buried as an extra guard, and gave him a starting role as a forward, which created a Hall-of-Fame career.

His funniest moment came at the season's most critical moment. In double-overtime in Game 7 of the NBA Finals, down by two points with two seconds left, Hannum called a play for himself. He would throw the ball the length of the court off the backboard and expect Bob Pettit to catch the carom and put it in?! Easy, right? It actually happened, and Pettit just rolled it off the rim, ending the championship quest. Slater Martin quipped, "We were in shock because Alex couldn't throw a ball in the ocean! Most of the time he couldn't hit the backboard from ten feet, but I'll be darned if he didn't do exactly what he said he would do. Now that's a good coach!"

The rest was history. Hannum left the Hawks after a remarkable 1957–58 season, winning the Western Division title and beating the favored Boston Celtics of Bill Russell and company in six games. In a stunning development, owner Ben Kerner let Hannum go when he wouldn't give the great coach a $2,000 raise. It may have cost the Hawks one or more future championships as Hannum went on to a Hall-of-Fame coaching career, winning again in 1967 with the Philadelphia 76ers. He was inducted in the Hall in 1998.

COACH "RED" HOLZMAN

YEARS WITH THE HAWKS: 2-PLUS SEASONS,
1954–MID-1956

Red Holzman was a player before he was a coach. He was a solid contributor on the floor for the 1950–51 NBA Champion Rochester Royals. He teamed with Bob Davies and Al Cervi in the Royals' only championship season. He earned his Hall-of-Fame stature, inducted in 1988, after he left the Hawks in 1956. Holzman had four tough seasons to begin his coaching career, including two last-place finishes in Milwaukee.

However, he began the development of Bob Pettit by putting the rookie on the floor from day one and leaving him there to earn his stripes. It paid off in Pettit's NBA Rookie-of-the-Year performance and a spot on the NBA All-Pro team.

Holzman was a class act who cared about his players and enjoyed the move to St. Louis from a dismal Milwaukee experience. That first regular-season third-place finish of 33–39 was promising. Then the postseason first-round victory over the Minneapolis Lakers followed by a hard-fought best of five series loss in Game 5 to Ft. Wayne gave the city great hope.

With thoughts of winning the Western Division Championship in the

1956–57 campaign, theseason got off to a rocky start. The lineup of Charlie Share, Bob Pettit, Ed Macauley, Slater Martin, and Jack McMahon created a high-powered offense with high expectations. However, the Hawks were struggling at 14–19 when the trigger finger of Kerner got itchy and he fired Holzman as coach.

"Red" thanked Kerner for the opportunity, and he used the experience to lead the New York Knicks to three NBA Finals appearances from 1970 to 1973, winning the championship twice. He posted 696 career coaching victories and was given the unofficial title of "Comeback Coach of the Century."

Coach Red Holzman fronts his starting five.

COACH HARRY GALLATIN

YEARS WITH THE HAWKS:
2-PLUS SEASONS, 1962–MID-1965

Harry Gallatin has often been left off lists of Hawks heroes, but he certainly played a positive role in team history and was one of the NBA's all-time greats. Gallatin isn't a member of the Hall of Fame as a Hawks coach because, while he did an excellent job for two-and-a-half seasons behind the bench, he's in the Hall of Fame as a power forward for the New York Knicks and Detroit Pistons.

A native of Wood River, Illinois, graduate of Northeast Missouri State, and former head coach of SIU–Carbondale, Harry was one of the "iron men" of professional basketball. He began as a Knick in 1948, playing for 10 seasons, including 682 consecutive games and 64 straight playoff games. He averaged 13 points and 11 rebounds per game, played in 8 All-Star Games, and earned 1 NBA First Team designation in 1954.

He took the Hawks coaching reins out of the college ranks and immediately turned a loser into a

winner. The 51 losses of the 1961–62 season were fresh when the tough, disciplined Gallatin restruc

tured the Hawks' style. With some new players like Chico Vaughn (from SIU) and John Barnhill joining Len Wilkens in the backcourt, the Hawks regained their confidence. The result was a 30–7 record at Kiel and a 48–32 overall mark for second place behind the Lakers.

Gallatin's gallant club beat Detroit in round one but lost the battle in seven tough games against the prohibitive favorite Los Angeles Lakers in the league finals. Still, Gallatin had brought respectability and exciting basketball back to Hawks fans, and Harry was rightfully named NBA Coach of the Year.

His second year, the 1963–64 season, had similar results, with Harry's "horses" posting a 42–38 second-place mark, another first-round victory over Detroit, and a conference finals defeat this time at the hands of the regular-season champion San Francisco Warriors. The Warriors were led by the towering infernos, Wilt Chamberlain and Nate Thurmond, but it still took seven games to knock out the Hawks. Unfortunately and ironically, the winning Warriors head coach should have been on the other bench—Alex Hannum.

The 1964–65 season doomed Gallatin behind the Hawks' bench. Riddled with early season injuries and a declining Cliff Hagan now coming off the bench, St. Louis was just 17–16 when Kerner got the itch and changed coaches again in midstream. Gallatin was replaced by guard Richie Guerin and another brief but successful coaching stint ended.

Gallatin went on to coach in New York for a couple of years before retiring back to St. Louis.

Bill Bridges

7 Colorful Characters and Fan Favorites

The St. Louis Hawks had their fair share of Hall-of-Famers, but a number of St. Louis Hawks endeared themselves to St. Louis fans. Without these players, the Hawks just wouldn't have been the Hawks. Whether it was a nickname, style, or heroic moment, generations of fans from the 1950s and 1960s retain fond memories of these players.

Buddy Blattner and Elgin Baylor

St. Louis Hawks 1965–66 team. Front row, L to R: Gene Washington, Mike Farmer, Zelmo Beaty, Gene Tormohlen, Joe Caldwell, Paul Silas. Back row, L to R: Trainer Fred Franz, Richie Guerin, John Barnhill, Len Wilkens, Cliff Hagan, Bill Bridges, Jeff Mullins, and Chico Vaughn.

ZELMO BEATY

1962–1968

At 6-9 "Big Z" was
a rock in the middle
of the Hawks lineup for
six seasons in St. Louis. He
played four seasons without
missing a regular-season game,
and twice he averaged 20 or more
points per game. Coach Richie
Guerin called Beaty "one of the
hardest workers he was ever
around and a slick-shooting pivot
man." Beaty once scored 30 points
against the Boston Celtics.

"JUMPIN'" JOE CALDWELL

1966–1968

A 6-5 forward-guard in St. Louis, Caldwell put a needed "charge" into the sagging Hawks in 1966. Acquired at a significant cost by trading John Barnhill and Chico Vaughn to Detroit, Caldwell's tremendous leaping ability and quickness could ignite rallies and the crowd alike. He was sensational in the 1966 playoffs when the Hawks unexpectedly swept the Baltimore Bullets 3–0 in the first round and took the mighty L.A. Lakers to the final minutes of Game 7 of the Conference Finals before losing. He averaged 18 points per game in the series and scored a then career high 33 points in Game 1 at Baltimore.

"Jumpin'" Joe was the spark that got the club going, always averaging in double figures, and he was a tough defender. He won an Olympic Gold Medal in 1964 in Tokyo.

AL FERRARI

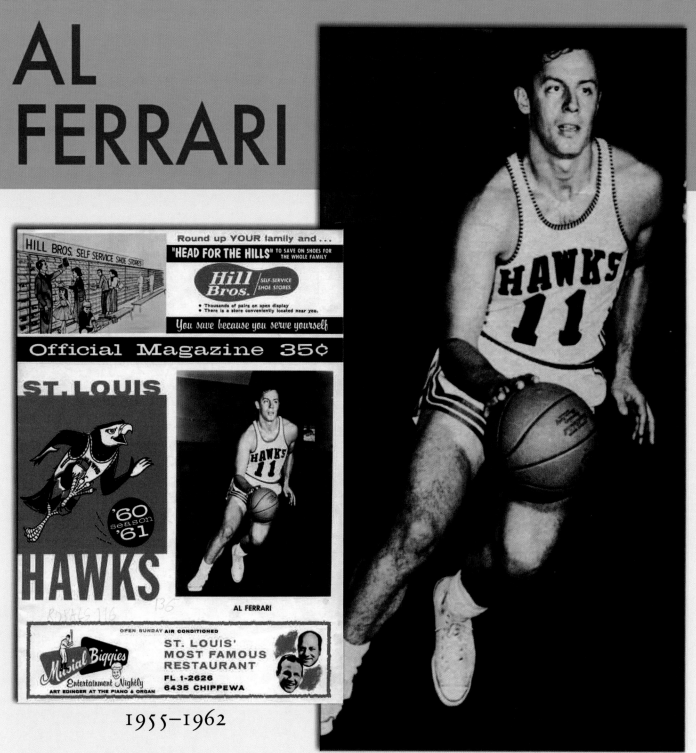

1955–1962

"Muggsy" or "Bronco," take your pick, Ferrari was a strong influence on the floor, particularly for his first two seasons. Sadly, he missed the championship year because of military duty, but Ferrari was always a spark off the bench at the guard position. He posted many games with 20 or more points and had a career high 34 points in a December 2, 1959, game against the Syracuse Nationals.

Led by Ferrari and Bob Pettit, the Hawks rallied from 19 points down in the third quarter of their first ever playoff game in Minneapolis to win a shocking 116–115 road game. Ferrari had 22 points, which included a driving layup in the closing minute to go with Pettit's two pressure free throws in the big win.

Ferrari's outstanding play in the 1955–56 playoffs helped secure St. Louis's first ever playoff game and series wins. He averaged 33 minutes of playing time and produced 15 points per game.

LARRY FOUST

1960–1962

A practical joker off the court, a fierce competitor on it, Foust filled a huge void at center when team captain Charlie Share was traded. At 6-9 and 240 lbs. and nicknamed "Large Lawrence," he had 10 seasons under his belt, 7 at Ft. Wayne and almost 3 at Minneapolis, before coming to the River City. His lifetime average of almost 14 points per game tells the story of a scorer who could rebound as well.

The Hawks lost Game 7 to the Boston Celtics in the 1959–60 season under Coach Ed Macauley, who says that had Foust not been hobbled by a healing broken hand and a terrible heel injury, then he may have been able to help slow Hall-of-Fame center Bill Russell. Foust retired as a St. Louis Hawk in 1962.

SIHUGO GREEN

1959–1962

Good guy Si Green, Al Ferrari's room-mate on the road, was a good clutch player. He was known for his defense, with modest success on offense, though changing from a college forward to a pro guard was difficult for him.

Ironically, Green was drafted No. 1 in the country by the Rochester Royals instead of San Francisco star Bill Russell in 1956, as an All-American from Duquesne. Of course, St. Louis had the second pick that year and thought Russell would go to Rochester, and they would have the rights to Green, everybody's second pick, which they had already agreed to trade to the Celtics for Macauley. Instead, the Hawks traded the rights to Russell for Macauley and Cliff Hagan.

Green's most important night as a Hawk came against the Minneapolis Lakers in Game 7 of the 1960 Conference Finals. He banged in 16 points with an amazing 13 assists while subbing for the great guard Slater Martin, who was out of the series with injuries. The Hawks advanced to the NBA Finals for the third time, winning 97–86. Green was the only African American on the team and was a player favorite.

RICHIE GUERIN

1964–1967

Guerin had a Hall-of-Fame career long before he came to St. Louis. He played three-plus seasons and coached over three years in the Gateway City. He scored over 10,000 points in just over seven seasons as a New York Knick, including 39 points, a forgotten stat, the night Philadelphia's Wilt Chamberlain scored 100 points against Guerin's club. The final score of that memorable game was Philadelphia 169, New York 147.

Player-coach Guerin breathed new life into the Hawks, leading the team in Pettit's final injury-plagued season to a

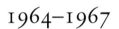

45–35 record by going 26–19 after taking over in 1964–65. Guerin led the Hawks to their best regular-season record ever in 1967–68, overcoming rumors of the team moving and injuries. They went 56–29 after a 16–1 start, winning the Western Division by a whopping 16 games. However, they were stunned in the playoffs, four games to two, by the San Francisco Warriors, the third place team.

Guerin continued to coach the Hawks another four seasons in Atlanta, giving him the longevity record to this day for the Tri-Cities, Milwaukee, St. Louis, Atlanta franchise.

LOU HUDSON

1966–1968

"Sweet Lou" Hudson was the next superstar of the Hawks in St. Louis after the departure of Pettit and Hagan. The Hawks' No. 1 pick and the league's fourth overall in 1966, Guerin called him "one of the greatest shooters in NBA history right there with West and Baylor." St. Louis fans got only two seasons with this remarkable talent, who made six straight NBA All-Star Teams in Atlanta.

Hudson had one of the league's premier jump shots and averaged 20 points per game over his career. He had games of 41 and 57 (tying Bob Pettit for a single game) as a St. Louis Hawk. He narrowly missed, finishing second, in the 1967 NBA Rookie-of-the-Year voting.

Hudson's finest moments in St. Louis came in the final third of his rookie season. He boosted his points per game average to 18, breaking Pettit's rookie-season record.

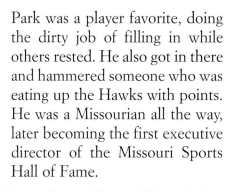

Park was a player favorite, doing the dirty job of filling in while others rested. He also got in there and hammered someone who was eating up the Hawks with points. He was a Missourian all the way, later becoming the first executive director of the Missouri Sports Hall of Fame.

MED PARK

1955–1959

At 6-2 and 205 lbs., the scrappy, gritty "bull-dozer from Missouri," Park was an original St. Louis Hawk and was an invaluable cog in the championship wheel. Park's play wasn't about stats. He played hard all the time and could wake up a slumbering team and crowd. His hustling play was his trademark, and he relished cutting taller, bigger opponents down to size.

CHARLIE SHARE

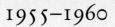

1955–1960

An "original Hawk" coming from Milwaukee with Bob Pettit, the 6-11 first pick in the NBA draft from Bowling Green University was the anchor and captain of the World Champions as the center. The scoring machines Pettit, Hagan, and Macauley relied on those solid screens and his tough lane play to protect them.

Share could score points as well. Always in the 10–12 point range, he kept the defense honest when it would want to double up Pettit and Hagan. He was named team captain, as he had the respect of his teammates and team owner and decision-maker Ben Kerner.

Share laughs that he would have scored more if he had been able to "play more fourth quarters instead of fouling out," but that was his style, and it paid dividends. At the final buzzer of the Hawks' championship win in 1958, after teammate Ed Macauley threw the basketball high into the Kiel Auditorium rafters, who caught it as the delirious crowd rushed onto the court? Charlie Share, and he hugged the ball all the way to the locker room!

PAUL SILAS

1964–1968

The burly Silas became a perennial NBA star over a stretch of seven seasons, which began with Phoenix and ended in championship seasons with Boston. In his tenure with the Hawks—four years—Silas learned his trade.

He improved each season, and by his fourth in St. Louis, he bumped up his totals to almost 12 rebounds and 13 points per game. He played alongside the workhorse up front for those years, Bill Bridges. That best season was the Hawks' last in St. Louis, so his contributions figured significantly into that 56-win Western Division Championship.

Who would have thought the Paul Silas of 1964 would survive and thrive for an amazing 17 seasons on just four NBA teams? He earned two championship rings with the Celtics, in 1973 and 1976.

CHICO VAUGHN

1962–1966

Already familiar to St. Louisans as a star collegian at SIU–Carbondale, Vaughn was coached at Southern Illinois by Hawks Coach Harry Gallatin. Vaughn started alongside John Barnhill and Lenny Wilkens and could be counted on for about 10 points per game and solid defense.

Vaughn was a reliable performer who had a memorable long-armed jump shot. He was a hard worker on the floor in the tradition of great Hawks teams, and he was eventually traded to Detroit in the deal that brought Joe Caldwell to St. Louis.

ADDITIONAL CHARACTERS
AND FAN FAVORITES

JOHN BARNHILL
(1962–1965)

Nicknamed "The Rabbit" for his great speed, Barnhill was a defensive standout who could score with a long one-handed shot that resembled a knuckleball in flight. In his first season, he scored 901 points—which averaged to be 11 points per game. He was traded to Detroit with Chico Vaughn and John Tresvant for Joe Caldwell during the 1965–66 season.

MARTY BLAKE
PUBLIC RELATIONS DIRECTOR
& GENERAL MANAGER

Colorful doesn't do justice to Marty's flamboyant style. A pioneer in NBA player scouting, he found great players to draft or sign in places other teams didn't even look. One outstanding example was Zelmo Beaty, who Blake had discovered even before he went to college at little Prairie View A&M. He also helped convince owner Ben Kerner that future Hall-of-Famer Lenny Wilkens was worth taking as their No. 1 choice. Blake also was a promotion king, bringing incredible talent like Guy Lombardo and the Count Basie Orchestra to entertain after games. Blake's esteem around the NBA kept him employed in the league for over 40 years.

BILL BRIDGES
(1962–1968)

A bruiser on the backboards, Bridges averaged 12 to 15 rebounds per game throughout his career. Bridges could be relied on to pound the boards and his opponents nightly. The burly 6-6 forward brought bulk and tenacity to the position from Kansas. His blue-collar approach to playing garnered the fans' attention.

JACK COLEMAN
(1949–1958)

Called "The Old Rancher" because of his rugged looks and his horse farm in Kentucky, Coleman came to the Hawks after a stellar six-plus years with the Rochester Royals. In the 1950–51 season, he averaged 11 points per game as an impor-tant part of the Royals' first and only NBA Championship.

As a Hawk for most of three seasons, he both started and subbed at the forward position, averaging 10 to 12 points per game, many of them key ones. He kept championship hopes alive in the 1956–57 Finals at Boston in the first overtime of Game 7 by hitting a game-tying shot around big Bill Russell at the buzzer. Coleman brought a talented shot and great savvy to a team that needed those ingredients and that depth in the 1957–58 season.

MIKE FARMER
(1962–1966)

Quiet but steady, Farmer logged substantial playing time for Coaches Gallatin and Guerin. A reliable and durable sub, Farmer contributed valuable minutes and got a half dozen points and several rebounds over the course of each game.

Farmer was a hard-working forward and just one of those many role players that gave the stars some breathing time on the bench, while he kept up the pace on the court.

JACK MCMAHON
(1956–1960)

A ruddy, red-faced man, built tough and sturdy, he was rock solid in the backcourt of the championship team. Another Rochester capture, "Jack Mac" got his eight points with that famous two-handed set shot, plus four or five assists per game while playing tenacious defense. McMahon played in the shadow of Dugie Martin, but he was a playmaker and the perfect complement.

McMahon logged a lot of minutes with the Hawks and put up plenty of assists. In Game 5 of the 1957–58 Championship Series with Boston, his work on defense went under the radar. He held the high-scoring Hall-of-Fame guard Bill Sharman to just 13 points in the Boston Garden in the tense 102–100 win that allowed the Hawks to play for the NBA Championship and win it in Game 6.

McMahon used that game knowledge to become an excellent NBA coach for the Cincinnati Royals, San Diego Rockets, and Chicago Zephyrs.

FAN-tastic!

WOODY SAULDSBERRY
(1960–1962)

Those who saw Woody swear he was a Hawk longer than the year and a half he played over two stints with the club. His famous slingshot, line-drive jump shot was unforgettable. Sauldsberry was an imposing man at 6-7 and 220 lbs. He had his best years in Philadelphia, where he averaged 12 and 15 points per game in two seasons.

Woody's high mark in St. Louis was the 1960–61 playoff run to the Finals when he averaged 13.7 points per game, scoring 164 points in the 12 contests. This former NBA Rookie of the Year was, according to the *Press Guide,* responsible for the Hawks edging the Los Angeles Lakers in the Western Division Finals, a breathtaking 105–103 Game 7 win at Kiel that sent St. Louis to the NBA Finals.

GENE TORMOHLEN
(1962–1968)

Everyone remembers "The Bumper," as big Gene was dubbed in St. Louis. His 6-9, 250-lb. frame was a nightmare for opponents, as he mostly played backup center to the Big Z, Zelmo Beaty, for six seasons. He was acquired at midseason after Clyde Lovellette was traded. He had come from the Cleveland Pipers, one of the top amateur teams in the nation, where he averaged 14 points and 15 rebounds per game.

Tormohlen could incite the Kiel crowd with his big hits against the big bodies of the opposing NBA players. He was to the Hawks what Jungle Jim Loscutoff was to Boston. Players like Pettit and Hagan appreciated his presence as a reminder not to mess with them or you may face the wrath of "The Bumper." There were brains with that brawn, rest assured, as Tormohlen later became an assistant coach to Richie Guerin.

WIN WILFONG
(1957–1959)

Though he played just two seasons in St. Louis, Win made an impact with fans and teammates alike. One of the best high school players in Missouri history, he only played four seasons in the NBA.

He was a guard who was a "ball hawk" with speed. Wilfong finished runner-up to Sauldsberry to NBA Rookie-of-the-Year honors as a member of the Hawks' World Champions. He was an aggressive player who'd drive the lane for the basket.

The original eight National Basketball Association owners.

8 THE COACHES CHRONOLOGY

This is the part of the story that defies logic. As perceptive as he was at making player trades and as imaginative as he was at game marketing, the Hawks' daring and aggressive owner Ben Kerner was a success at selecting head coaches as well, but he did fail to keep the good ones. Ten different men held the title of coach over the 13 seasons in St. Louis.

The main culprit for the flaw was his philosophy about coaching. He didn't profess to know anything about the profession, but he felt strongly about one thing—they weren't very important, and for sure they were not bigger than him with regards to the ball club. These were Ben's boys.

His friend and press-table guru Jack Levitt remembers, "It wasn't that he'd say they're not important, but in the way he handled the team and the way he handled the coach you could tell he didn't think that position was important. Ben would say, 'I've got Pettit, I've got Hagan, I've got Martin, I've got Macauley. Heck I could coach them and win.' He wouldn't ever give coaches any credit."

So considering those facts, here is the litany of coaches that ownership ran through in 13 seasons in St. Louis. One footnote: In the combined six previous seasons at Tri-Cities and in Milwaukee, the Hawks passed through eight head coaches including Hall-of-Famer Arnold "Red" Auerbach!

WILLIAM RED HOLZMAN
1955–1956, 1956–1957 (33 GAMES)
RECORD: 47–58

Red came with the Hawks from Milwaukee where he survived two last-place finishes. The team finished third in the Western Division ahead of Rochester the first season in St. Louis, and they upset Minneapolis in the first round of the playoffs for St. Louis's first taste of success.

High expectations to compete for the title the second year were not being met, and Red was fired with a record of 14–19. Give him credit for one thing—if the Hawks hadn't finished last in the 1953–54 season, they wouldn't have had the No. 1 draft pick, which brought No. 9 Bob Pettit to the Hawks.

SLATER MARTIN
1956–1957 (EIGHT GAMES)
RECORD: 5–3

Martin was named head coach to replace Red Holzman, and he took the job kickin' and scratchin'. He didn't want the position to compromise his playing time on the floor, where he thought he might be able to lead a now-talented team up the ladder in the NBA. "It was the last thing I wanted to do, play and coach," Martin shook his head. "I told Kerner he had a guy on the team whose best playing days were behind him but who had the discipline to be an excellent head coach. I knew Ben didn't like the guy, but I told him the players did and he was the right man—Alex Hannum."

ALEX HANNUM
1956–1957, 1957–1958
RECORD: 56–47
ONE NBA CHAMPIONSHIP

Hannum had started the season playing for Ft. Wayne, was acquired as a player for a second tour

Andy Phillip

with the Hawks, and suddenly was named the team's third head coach of the season in January. Ed Macauley recalls Hannum had an immediate positive effect on a team whose heads were swimming with the lack of continuity in management. He was a hard-nosed, no-nonsense guy, and he had few plays but expected everybody to go hard every minute on the court.

Hannum's year-and-a-half were the most exciting in Hawks history. Though they were only 15–16 with him the rest of the first year, it was enough to win a weak Western Division. The fiery "Old Sarge," as he was called, had stabilized the lineup, found a new star in Cliff Hagan, and had a relaxed Slater Martin leading the charge down the floor. Then of course, he had Bob Pettit pouring in the points and piling up the rebounds.

His Hawks came within two points in double overtime of winning the NBA title in Boston. The drastically underdog Hawks scared the Celtics right down to the last play when player-coach Hannum heaved the ball the length of

the floor, off the backboard, and into the surprised grasp of Pettit who just had his buzzer-beater attempt roll off the rim.

The following season, Hannum guided the club to a solid 41–31 first-place finish. This time the Hawks finished off the Celtics in six games, winning the World Championship at Kiel. Then in the usual unpredictable fashion, Hannum was let go as head coach because Kerner would not give in to a small raise request.

ANDY PHILLIP
1958–1959 (10 GAMES)
RECORD: 6–4

The bewildered Hawks fans saw Phillip arrive and were told he was a local guy—Granite City. He was soft spoken and a 12-year veteran of the league, but he had never coached anyone in his life, not exactly credentials to lead the defending World Champions.

It didn't matter, because this time Kerner "didn't like the way the team was winning," and when Phillip showed up late for a game, he was fired the next day.

"EASY" ED MACAULEY
1958–1959 (62 GAMES), 1959–1960
RECORD: 89–42
ONE NBA FINAL

St. Louis' favorite son Ed Macauley was another coach who didn't apply for the job. He too was playing on the defending champions when called into the office and offered the option of retirement, a trade, or the head coaching job?! Give the man the clipboard. He became an outstanding success for another short tenure, starting with a franchise-best 43–19 the rest of the season. The St. Louis Hawks went 49–23, won the West, and were favored to repeat as champs. However, the Minneapolis Lakers jumped up and surprised St. Louis by beating them in six games in the Conference Finals.

The second season went just as well for Macauley, with a regular-season record of 46–29. This time his team won the first round and then rallied from a 3–2 deficit on the road at Minneapolis by winning Game 6 away and Game 7 at Kiel to head back to the NBA Finals for the third time. Battling injuries at center, the Hawks couldn't get by the explosive Celtics, losing in Game 7 at the Boston Garden after a heroic struggle.

Macauley was a coaching hero to the players and fans alike, bringing them back into the championship round. But the trigger-happy Kerner was unimpressed. He had committed an unpardonable sin of secretly hiring a new coach for the next season before Game 6 of the semi-finals, thinking his team would lose and bow out. Macauley was gone after setting a mark of wins as a coach, a .650 winning percentage that has never been eclipsed to this day by a St. Louis or Atlanta Hawks coach.

PAUL SEYMOUR
1960–1961, 1961–1962 (14 GAMES)
RECORD: 56–37
ONE NBA FINAL

A good guy put in a tough spot replacing fan-favorite and highly successful Macauley, at least Seymour came with experience from the Syracuse Nationals, where he coached four years. He also inherited a great ensemble in Pettit, Hagan, and Clyde Lovellette up front and now a young promising star Lenny Wilkens to replace the retired Slater Martin.

Seymour got the Hawks rolling, and they romped to the Western Division title with the first 50-win season, 51–28. Their dominating 16-game lead over the Lakers in the regular season didn't matter, and in the Conference Finals it took seven games to knock out Los Angeles. Seymour's tired Hawks were beaten in six games again by Boston in the Finals.

Once again, winning didn't mean much the second season, and after just 14 games and a 5–9 record, Seymour was let go. This time the players were unhappy that the coach had chosen to play an untested rookie, and there was some unrest in the locker room.

ANDREW FUZZY LEVANE
1961–1962 (60 GAMES)
RECORD: 20–40

Levane, a former player-coach with the Milwaukee Hawks, returned for a second stint with the franchise. Levane, it turned out, brought nothing to stop the bleeding, and St. Louis had the worst season in the city's history, ending at a miserable 29–51. Levane was let go mercifully with six games to play.

BOB PETTIT
1961–1962 (6 GAMES)
RECORD: 4–2

Proving he could truly do it all in the game of pro basketball, Pettit bowed to the wishes of Mr. Kerner and agreed to be the coach of the team for the final six games of the season. There were not going to be any playoffs this year, so the stress level of the job was not going to bring on any migraines for Big Blue. He did get to brag that he went in and out a winner!

HARRY GALLATIN
1962–1963, 1963–1964, 1964–1965 (33 GAMES)
RECORD: 111–82

It should be recognized here first that Harry "The Horse" Gallatin is not listed on the Hawks' Hall-of-Fame list because he was a coach for them, but he earned his Hall-of-Fame ring as a player for the New York Knickerbockers. He was one of the NBA's all-time greats, known for his durability, rebounding, and rugged play.

As a coach, he became St. Louis's first NBA Coach of the Year in his first year. Gallatin lead the Hawks to a 48–32 record, good for second place behind the superb talents of Elgin Baylor, Jerry West, and the Los Angeles Lakers, who won 53 games. The favored Lakers won the Western Division in seven games, helped by injuries to Cliff Hagan and Zelmo Beaty.

The second year, Gallatin's troops finished second again at 46–34, but this time ahead of the faltering Lakers. Instead, the upstart San Francisco Warriors were at the top. They were led by the twin towers, Wilt Chamberlain and Nate Thurmond, a pair of seven footers. The Warriors, ironically coached by Alex Hannum, waged a bitter dual with the Hawks and defeated St. Louis 4–3. The Warriors had upset the Hawks at Kiel, which spelled the difference.

Gallatin's third and final season started badly, as the injury-riddled Hawks were 17–16 when the recently acquired Richie Guerin, a superstar in New York, became the player-coach on December 27, 1964.

RICHIE GUERIN
1964–1965 THROUGH 1967–1968
RECORD: 159–131

Guerin ended up as the longest-running coach of the Hawks in St. Louis, and he carried forward as their head coach for four more seasons in Atlanta. His team finished up the 1964–65 season in fine style, going 28–19 after the coaching switch for a 45–35 mark.

However, with Pettit retired and Hagan limited to coming off the bench, a new era had begun and a new team had to be built. The new players joining Wilkens and Beaty were Bill Bridges, Joe Caldwell, Chico Vaughn, John Barnhill, and eventually the magnificent shooter "Sweet" Lou Hudson. Guerin also continued to play and coach.

Coach Richie Guerin

In the final season in St. Louis, Guerin's club jelled, bolting out to a 16–1 start. After a franchise record of 56 wins, the team regained Hawks pride by winning the Western Division. Unfortunately, it was too late, and the fans had split their loyalties between hockey and basketball. An upset loss to San Francisco in the playoffs was the quiet ending of the Hawks in St. Louis.

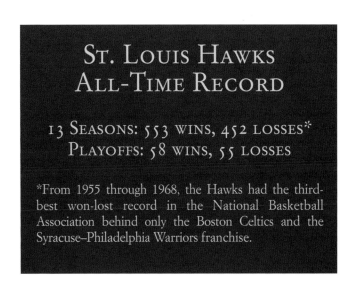

ST. LOUIS HAWKS ALL-TIME RECORD

13 SEASONS: 553 WINS, 452 LOSSES*
PLAYOFFS: 58 WINS, 55 LOSSES

*From 1955 through 1968, the Hawks had the third-best won-lost record in the National Basketball Association behind only the Boston Celtics and the Syracuse–Philadelphia Warriors franchise.

9 The NBA All-Star Games Played in St. Louis

69—The Arena, St. Louis, Mo.

This section is a tribute to the city and the fans of St. Louis. The NBA of the 1950s was a new league fighting for respectability and an audience across the country. Of the eight franchises in the league when the Hawks put down their stakes in St. Louis in 1955, nobody was close to selling out their buildings. The Boston Celtics were among the worst, with only a few thousand fans in attendance most nights, making the Boston Garden a giant echo chamber.

But in just the second season, St. Louis was drawing close to capacity for big games and began filling their 10,000 seats for playoffs and Celtics games. Starting with the championship season, sellouts were the order of the day for the vibrant Hawks, and on the road, they were one of the NBA's biggest draws, with Bob Pettit and Cliff Hagan heading the marquee.

For these reasons, the NBA owners were happy to select St. Louis three times in just seven years to host the NBA All-Star Game. Because St. Louisans would buy the tickets, the All-Star Games were not played at the Hawks' home court, Kiel, but were moved out to Oakland Avenue in the spacious St. Louis Arena. Two non–St. Louis games are listed in this chapter, because Bob Pettit was named Most Valuable Player in these contests.

JANUARY 21, 1958
EAST 130, WEST 118
ELGIN BAYLOR DRIVING TO THE BASKET
WINNING COACH: RED AUERBACH (BOSTON)
LOSING COACH: ALEX HANNUM (ST. LOUIS)
MOST VALUABLE PLAYER: BOB PETTIT (ST. LOUIS) 28 PTS., 26 REBOUNDS
ATTENDANCE — 12,854

JANUARY 21, 1958
EAST 130, WEST 118
WILT CHAMBERLAIN SHOOTING RUNNING JUMP SHOT
WINNING COACH: RED AUERBACH (BOSTON)
LOSING COACH: ALEX HANNUM (ST. LOUIS)
MOST VALUABLE PLAYER: BOB PETTIT (ST. LOUIS) 28 PTS., 26 REBOUNDS
ATTENDANCE — 12,854

JANUARY 24, 1956
WEST 108, EAST 94
WINNING COACH: CHARLEY ECKMAN (DETROIT)
LOSING COACH: GEORGE SENESKY (PHILADELPHIA)
MOST VALUABLE PLAYER: BOB PETTIT (ST. LOUIS) 20 PTS., 24 REBOUNDS
ATTENDANCE—8,517

January 16, 1962
West 150, East 130
Winning Coach: Fred Schaus (Los Angeles)
Losing Coach: Red Auerbach (Boston)
Most Valuable Player: Bob Pettit (St. Louis) 25 pts., 27 rebounds
Attendance—15,112

January 13, 1965
East 124, West 123
Winning Coach: Red Auerbach (Boston)
Losing Coach: Alex Hannum (Philadelphia)
Most Valuable Player: Jerry Lucas (Cincinnati) 25 points
Attendance—16,713

St. Louis HAWKS

GEORGE MIKAN — Lakers

"OFFICIAL PROGRAM"

25¢

86

St. Louis was blessed to be a part of professional basketball's "golden era." The early days had just eight NBA franchises, which kept the level of play high every night. St. Louis professional basketball also was a part of the introduction of African American players, whose exciting style of play opened up the game.

The NBA mirrored Major League Baseball in the 1950s and 1960s, as both sports had a proliferation of great players whose accomplishments have survived the test of time. Going to Hawks games at Kiel was a steal for the $1.50 upper-deck and $4.50 courtside seats to see the sport's greatest athletes put on a show.

Imagine going to Kiel Auditorium on a Tuesday night for one price to see two NBA games with four teams in action! It happened regularly around the league. How about walking into Kiel at 5:30 p.m. to see the Philadelphia Warriors with Wilt Chamberlain and Paul Arizin play the Cincinnati Royals with Robertson, Jack Twyman and Wayne Embry? Then get ready for the second game at 8:30 p.m. when the host Hawks entertain the star attraction, the Boston Celtics, with Bill Russell, Bob Cousy, and Bill Sharman?

These were the teams and some of the superstars that caused the NBA to soar in popularity and caught fire with the fans of St. Louis.

NBA 1955 FRANCHISES

WESTERN DIVISION

MINNEAPOLIS LAKERS

FT. WAYNE PISTONS

ROCHESTER ROYALS

ST. LOUIS HAWKS

EASTERN DIVISION

PHILADELPHIA WARRIORS

SYRACUSE NATIONALS

NEW YORK KNICKERBOCKERS

BOSTON CELTICS

BOB COUSY

The greatest playmaker and passer ever to play in St. Louis and possibly in all of NBA history, "Cooz" led the Celtics to six championships in seven years, losing only to the 1957–58 Hawks. He was a tremendous scorer as well, tallying 16,960 points in his career and once pouring in 50 points in an NBA playoff game.

A 13-time All-Star winning MVP honors in 1954 and 1957, he was NBA MVP in 1957. Cousy's floor battles with the Hawks' Hall-of-Fame guard Slater Martin during the 1950s were epic. Cousy said, "Martin is the only guy in the league I don't look forward to playing against, but we had great games together." Cousy was All-NBA First Team 10 years. Cousy was selected one of the greatest 50 players in NBA history in 1996.

BOSTON CELTICS

BACKCOURT
BOB COUSY

AMADEE

14

BILL RUSSELL

His presence stopped the Hawks from winning more NBA championships with his dominating defensive prowess. His shot-blocking ability, and just the threat of this ability, intimidated the opponent. His rebounding allowed the Celtics guards to fly down the court for a pass.

He won 11 championships in 13 seasons, grabbed 21,721 rebounds, averaged 15.1 points per game, appeared in 12 NBA All-Star Games with one MVP, and earned the NBA MVP Award five times. Russell was selected one of the NBA's greatest 50 players in 1996.

BOSTON
CELTICS

CENTER
BILL RUSSELL

89

OSCAR ROBERTSON

Probably the most versatile player in the history of the NBA, Robertson was a master at all phases of the game. In his second season in the league, he "averaged" a triple-double for the ENTIRE season! He averaged 30 points, 12 rebounds, and 11 assists per game.

Playing the Hawks didn't hurt his averages. He poured in 30 or more points per game in his years playing St. Louis. It was a treat to see the magnificent "Big O" cruise up and down the Kiel floor at will. His court sense was unmatched, which added to his style and grace on the floor, all of which characterized Oscar. He had an untouchable one-handed shot held over his head.

He was nine times First Team All-Pro, NBA Rookie of the Year, NBA MVP once, and 12-time All-Star. With three MVPs, his triple-double average for the season in 1962 is still the only one in the history of the game. He was elected to the Naismith Basketball Hall of Fame in 1979.

14

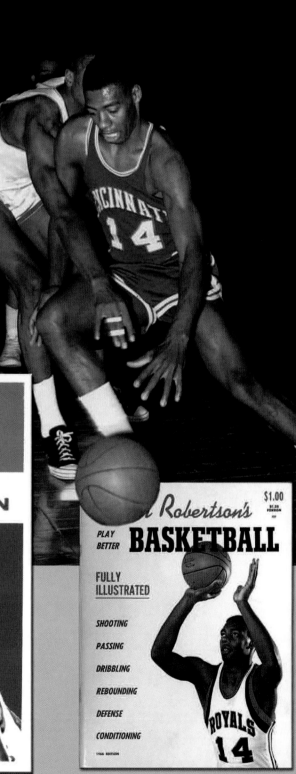

CINCINNATI ROYALS

**BACKCOURT
OSCAR ROBERTSON**

$1.00

Robertson's

PLAY
BETTER **BASKETBALL**

**FULLY
ILLUSTRATED**

SHOOTING

PASSING

DRIBBLING

REBOUNDING

DEFENSE

CONDITIONING

JERRY WEST

Hawks announcer Bud Blattner loved nicknames and would call out "Zeke from Cabin Creek," the hometown of the great No. 44 crew-cut guard from West Virginia. His prowess against the Hawks was legendary. In 1966–67, West averaged 31 points per game against St. Louis.

His arrival in Los Angeles created a major stumbling block for the Hawks in their efforts to win the Western Division and get back to the Finals. West and company knocked St. Louis out of the playoffs twice in the division finals, 1962–63 and 1965–66.

West got the Lakers to the NBA Finals nine of 13 seasons and was a First Team All-Pro selection ten times. Incredibly, the Lakers won the NBA championship only once during his tenure. He led the NBA in scoring, assists, and free throws made on different occasions, and in 1966, he averaged 40 points per game in the playoffs. He was inducted into the Hall of Fame in 1979.

JERRY WEST
SNAGS A REBOUND

FORWARD
JERRY WEST

44

DOLPH SCHAYES

He led the Nats to their one and only NBA title in 1955, the year the Hawks arrived in St. Louis. He was a shooter, playing nine years in Syracuse while averaging 17 points and 12 rebounds per game. He also shot an outstanding 84 percent from the free throw line for his career.

Schayes played 16 seasons in the league, and was a 12-time All-NBA First or Second Team member. He also had seasons where he averaged 21 or 22 points per game and three times led the league in free throw percentage. The Hawks had to stop Schayes to beat those competitive Nationals. Dolph Schayes is a 1972 Hall of Fame inductee.

SYRACUSE NATIONALS

DOLPH SCHAYES
SHOOTS

WILT CHAMBERLAIN

The most imposing offensive player in the history of professional basketball, Wilt "the Stilt" Chamberlain could dominate like no other. His battles with Bill Russell of Boston are epic and had plenty to do with the country's burgeoning interest in the NBA in the 1960s.

Chamberlain brought the "dunk" into basketball. He averaged 50.4 points per game for the 1961–62 season and 44 just two years later. For his car-eer, he was a 30-point-per-game man.

Obviously, he could rebound at his enormous 7'1", 275 lb. stature. He averaged 22 rebounds per game in his 14 seasons, leading the league on several occasions and almost always in the top three. He hit that average against the Hawks and the likes of Charlie Share, Larry Foust, and Bob Pettit.

His biggest claim to fame is the 100-point night on March 2, 1992, a game played in Hershey, Pennsylvania, and viewed by only 4,124 fans. Philadelphia beat New York, 169–147, and nobody paid attention to future Hawks player-coach Richie Guerin's 39-point performance. Wilt was 36 for 63 from the field, and an amazing 28 for 32 from the foul line. By quarters, the Big Dipper scored 23, 18, 28 and 31 for 100.

PHILADELPHIA WARRIORS

CENTER
WILT CHAMBERLAIN

ELGIN BAYLOR

LOS ANGELES LAKERS

FORWARD
ELGIN BAYLOR

Baylor was the closest to Michael Jordan in ability to drive, dish, or shoot while sailing through the air. Rookie of the Year and All-NBA First Team in 1959, he had that latter distinction a total of 10 times in his career.

Baylor clearly has the honor of being one of those superstars who paved the way and created a style for future stars to emulate, like Julius Irving, Michael Jordan, and Kobe Bryant, right up to LeBron James today.

Baylor versus Pettit was a fabulous matchup of scorers and rebounders, though Cliff Hagan drew the near-impossible assignment of stopping Baylor. He had that nervous twitch with his head that, while disconcerting to watch, was a great advantage when trying to fake out the opposition. He was co-MVP of the 1959 All-Star Game with Pettit. Baylor joined the Hall of Fame in 1976.

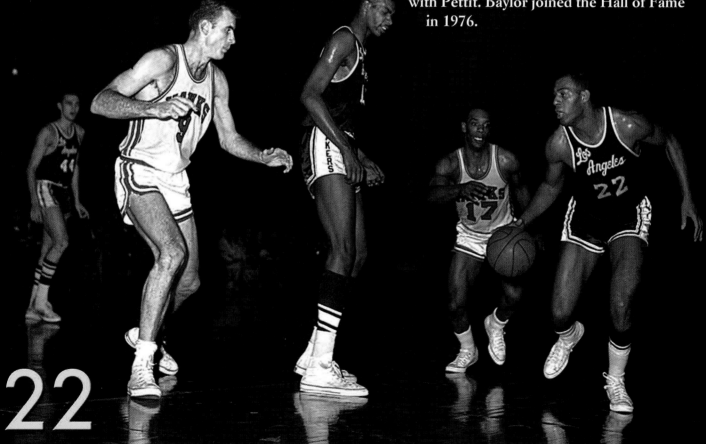

22

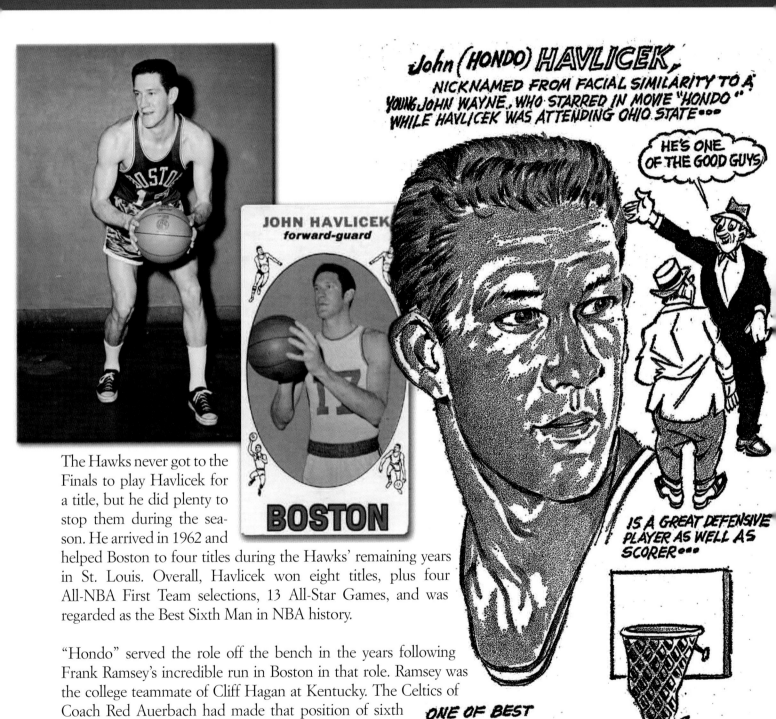

John (HONDO) HAVLICEK, NICKNAMED FROM FACIAL SIMILARITY TO A YOUNG JOHN WAYNE, WHO STARRED IN MOVIE "HONDO" WHILE HAVLICEK WAS ATTENDING OHIO STATE***

HE'S ONE OF THE GOOD GUYS

JOHN HAVLICEK
forward-guard

BOSTON

The Hawks never got to the Finals to play Havlicek for a title, but he did plenty to stop them during the season. He arrived in 1962 and helped Boston to four titles during the Hawks' remaining years in St. Louis. Overall, Havlicek won eight titles, plus four All-NBA First Team selections, 13 All-Star Games, and was regarded as the Best Sixth Man in NBA history.

"Hondo" served the role off the bench in the years following Frank Ramsey's incredible run in Boston in that role. Ramsey was the college teammate of Cliff Hagan at Kentucky. The Celtics of Coach Red Auerbach had made that position of sixth man famous.

Havlicek averaged close to 20 points per game, was a tremendous clutch player, and was inducted into the Hall of Fame in 1983.

IS A GREAT DEFENSIVE PLAYER AS WELL AS SCORER***

ONE OF BEST FREE THROW SHOOTERS IN LEAGUE WITH .833 MARK

TAKE ONE— THEY'RE FREE

17

AMADEE

GEORGE MIKAN
MINNEAPOLIS LAKERS
CENTER

The first "Big Man" in pro basketball history, Mikan played briefly at the end of his career when the Hawks arrived in St. Louis. His picture graced one of the first game programs at Kiel Auditorium. At 6-10 and 245 lbs., he was dominant. He led the Lakers to five titles in six years and had as his teammates two players who became vital to the Hawks, guard Slater Martin and center Clyde Lovellette.

Mikan led the NBA in scoring three times and rebounding once. He was selected as one of the 50 greatest players in NBA history in 1996.

PAUL ARIZIN
PHILADELPHIA WARRIORS
GUARD

He was always tough on the Hawks and averaged over 20 points per game for nine seasons, including 24.2 points per game in his Warriors championship 1956 season. A 10-time All-Star with one MVP, he led the NBA in scoring twice and was selected as one of the 50 greatest players in NBA history in 1996.

Great Players Who Entertained Hawks Faithful...

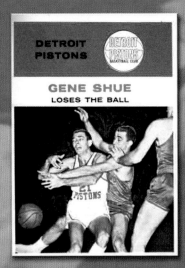

DETROIT PISTONS

GENE SHUE
LOSES THE BALL

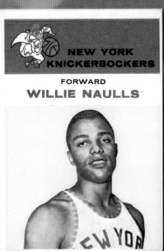

NEW YORK KNICKERBOCKERS

FORWARD
WILLIE NAULLS

Rick Barry (San Francisco)
Walt Bellamy (Chicago-Baltimore)
Bill Bradley (New York)
Dave DeBusschere (New York)
Hal Greer (Syracuse)
Tommy Heinsohn (Boston)
Bailey Howell (Detroit)
Neil Johnson (Philadelphia)
Sam Jones (Boston)
K.C. Jones (Boston)
Rudy LaRusso (Los Angeles)
Jerry Lucas (Cincinnati)
Willie Naulls (New York)
Guy Rodgers (San Francisco)
Maurice Stokes (Cincinnati)
Nate Thurmond (San Francisco)
Jack Twyman (Cincinnati)
George Yardley (Ft. Wayne-Detroit)

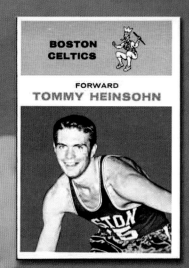

BOSTON CELTICS

FORWARD
TOMMY HEINSOHN

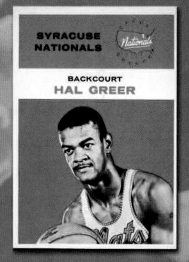

SYRACUSE NATIONALS

BACKCOURT
HAL GREER

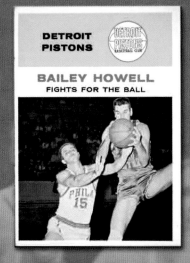

DETROIT PISTONS

BAILEY HOWELL
FIGHTS FOR THE BALL

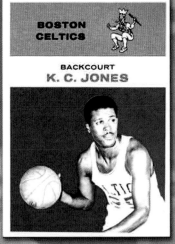

BOSTON CELTICS

BACKCOURT
K. C. JONES

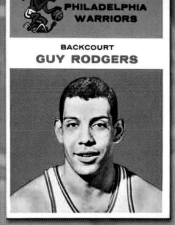

PHILADELPHIA WARRIORS

BACKCOURT
GUY RODGERS

CHICAGO PACKERS

CENTER
WALT BELLAMY

An award presentation made to Hawks' owner Ben Kerner for his service to the St. Louis community made by August A. Busch, Jr. (right) at the halftime of a Hawks game.

Some sports franchises couldn't find 20 spectacular moments in their history, even if the teams have been around 20, 30, or 40 years, much less just 13. But for the St. Louis Hawks, the difficulty was in narrowing down the moments. Without doubt, there are two moments that stand head-and-shoulders above all others. The first is the day the NBA allowed the franchise to move to St. Louis. The second is Pettit's 50 points to win the NBA Championship.

The thrilling moments in this chapter evoke personal memories for fans who can attach a story of a day with their dad or their friends and family watching the Hawks mount a comeback or win in the last seconds. These moments are the threads that wove the story of the Hawks.

Bob Pettit (left) and Cliff Hagan hold the World Championship Trophy prior to the 2005 Missouri Athletic Club dinner to celebrate the debut of Full Court: The Untold Stories of the St. Louis Hawks, *at which many of the former Hawks players were in attendance.*

1955

May 11, 1955—NBA approves the franchise transfer of the Milwaukee Hawks to St. Louis, and a new era of basketball begins.

November 5, 1955—The first regular season NBA game ever played in St. Louis at Kiel Auditorium between the St. Louis Hawks and Minneapolis Lakers, won by St. Louis, 101–89.

Milwaukee Hawks Shifted to St. Louis by NBA

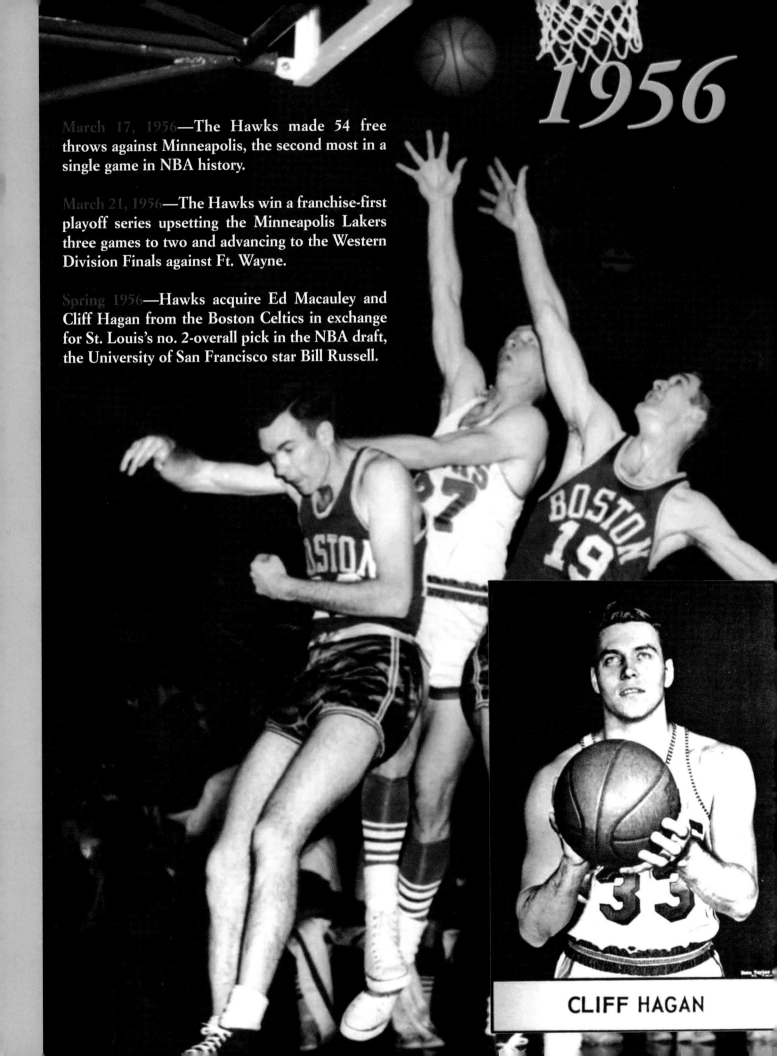

1956

March 17, 1956—The Hawks made 54 free throws against Minneapolis, the second most in a single game in NBA history.

March 21, 1956—The Hawks win a franchise-first playoff series upsetting the Minneapolis Lakers three games to two and advancing to the Western Division Finals against Ft. Wayne.

Spring 1956—Hawks acquire Ed Macauley and Cliff Hagan from the Boston Celtics in exchange for St. Louis's no. 2-overall pick in the NBA draft, the University of San Francisco star Bill Russell.

CLIFF HAGAN

March 16, 1957—A good-news, bad-news scenario occurs when superstar Bob Pettit breaks his wrist in a loss to Boston. It forced a reluctant Coach Red Holzman to insert first-year man Cliff Hagan into the lineup at forward. Hagan scored 17 and 16 points respectively in his first two games and was a consistent scoring leader the rest of the season.

March 25, 1957—The Hawks upend the Lakers in double overtime, 143–135, to sweep a best-of-five Western Division Finals series, advancing to the NBA Finals for the first time.

March 30, 1957—St. Louis shocks the heavily favored Boston Celtics in Game 1 at the Boston Garden, 125–123 in double overtime. Bob Pettit's 37 points and Ed Macauley's 23 points led to the victory.

April 13, 1957—Demonstrating great resolve, the Hawks finally succumb in double overtime at the Boston Garden in Game 7 of the NBA Finals, 125–123. The game ended with Alex Hannum's desperate attempt to tie it by throwing the ball the length of the court off the backboard for a Pettit tip-in.

April 1957—The Hawks and Celtics set a still-standing NBA record of having 10 players ejected in a seven-game playoff series during the Finals.

1958

March 29, 1958—The Hawks, after a superb regular season, rise again to beat the Celtics in Game 1 of the NBA Finals in Boston, 104–102, behind Hagan's 33 points.

April 12, 1958—St. Louis goes crazy after winning its first and only NBA Championship four games to two over Boston. Bob Pettit sets an NBA record by scoring 50 points to help win the title. Final score was 110–109.

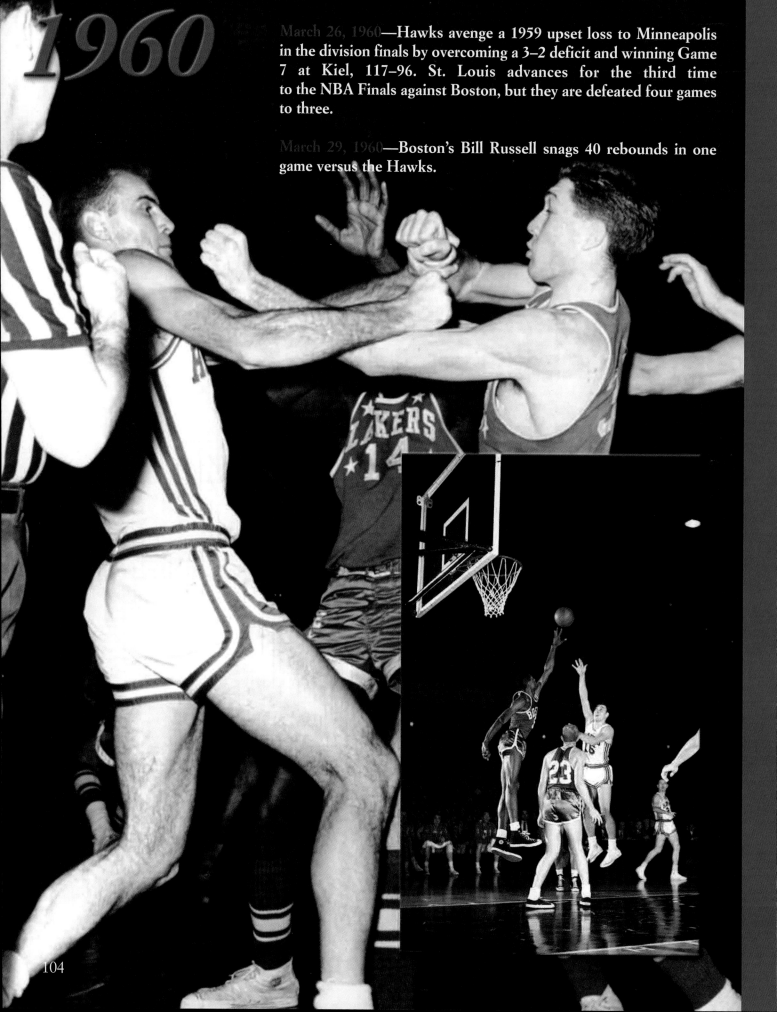

1960

March 26, 1960—Hawks avenge a 1959 upset loss to Minneapolis in the division finals by overcoming a 3–2 deficit and winning Game 7 at Kiel, 117–96. St. Louis advances for the third time to the NBA Finals against Boston, but they are defeated four games to three.

March 29, 1960—Boston's Bill Russell snags 40 rebounds in one game versus the Hawks.

1961

Spring 1961—The Hawks win a thrilling seven-game series for the Western Division title against the Lakers, 4–3. In Game 4, new guard standout Len Wilkens hits two free throws after the final buzzer had sounded to beat Los Angeles, 118–117. St. Louis won Game 7 in a nail-biter 105–103.

April 11, 1961—Boston ends the Hawks run for the championship in Game 5 at home, 121–112, in what would be St. Louis's last trip to the NBA Championship round.

1963

Season of 1963—Harry Gallatin, a future basketball Hall of Famer, is named NBA Coach of the Year for leading the revitalized Hawks back from their worst season ever (29–51) to a 48–32 second-place finish.

Season of 1963—The incomparable Bob Pettit announces his retirement after 10 Hall-of-Fame seasons, as injuries severely limit his playing time. He averaged 22 points per game, 4 below his career, playing just 50 games.

HOOPIN' AND HOLLERIN' STARTS TONIGHT

HAWKS COACH
Harry GALLATIN
EMPHASIZED DEFENSE AND HELPED CLUB MOVE FROM FOURTH PLACE IN 1961-62 TO CLOSE SECOND LAST SEASON...

SPENT 10 YEARS AS NBA PLAYER, MOSTLY WITH N.Y. KNICKS... COMPETED IN 682 CONSECUTIVE GAMES, EARNING NICKNAME 'HARRY THE HORSE'...

HARRY WON'T HOLD STILL FOR THE HORSE COLLAR

NAMED 'COACH OF YEAR' AFTER FIRST NBA SEASON WITH BEN KERNER'S CREW

1967-68

Season of 1967–68—Coach Richie Guerin's Hawks set a franchise record of 56 wins against just 26 defeats, edging out the favored L.A. Lakers for the regular-season Western title. "Sweet" Lou Hudson comes into his own as an NBA star, scoring 57 points in one game to tie Pettit's all-time single-game record set in 1961.

May 3, 1968—Owner Ben Kerner sells the Hawks to Atlanta interests Tom Cousins and former Georgia Governor Carl Sanders

LOU HUDSON
forward

St. Louis

Declining Attendance Cited

Hawks Team Sold to Atlanta

By JOHN J. ARCHIBALD
Of the Post-Dispatch Staff

A belief that he had a product that St. Louisans no longer wanted caused Ben Kerner to sell the Hawks to an Atlanta group Kerner said today.

The sale of the National Basketball Association club is effective immediately, pending approval of other NBA owners at a meeting Tuesday in New York. The purchasers are Thomas G. Cousins, a Georgia real estate developer, and former Gov. Carl E. Sanders. Kerner, who brought the Hawks to St. Louis from Mil-

waukee in the spring of 1955, cited disappointing attendance as his primary reason for disposing of the club.

No sale price was announced, but the Atlanta men are believed to have paid about $3,000,000. This was said to be the amount that Kerner was seeking last January when he made a public attempt to sell the club. When he did not receive a satisfactory offer, he took the Hawks off the market.

Cites Attendance Problem

Regarding the sale to Atlanta interests, Kerner said, "The attendance for the last four or

five years has not been good. It appears that the interest is not there.

"If you have a product that people don't want, you can't make them buy it."

Kerner said that the attendance at the Hawks games in St. Louis averaged "just about the same" in 1967-68 as it had the two previous seasons, despite promotion effort and great success by the team.

The Hawks, coached by Richie Guerin, won 16 of their first 17 games and held first place in the NBA's Western Division throughout the season. They

Hawks Started With 16-1

Crowds Discouraged Kerner

FROM PAGE ONE

Orleans group was reported to have completed a deal, but Kerner insisted that if a St. Louis group could match the price, he would perfer that the team remain here.

It soon developed that the New Orleans people were not so financially sound as they had originally indicated and the deal fell through. When no acceptable St. Louis offer was received, Kerner decided to keep the team himself.

The Hawks finished second in the Western Division in their first season in St. Louis, 1955-56.

The following season they won the first of five consecutive Western titles. St. Louis won the NBA playoff championship in 1958, beating the Boston Celtics.

Kerner said he was certain that the current purchasers had the resources to buy the team.

Cousins founded Cousins Properties Inc. in 1958 with a capitalization of $3000. The firm now lists assets of $14,000,000.

Hawks general manager Marty Blake has been asked to go to Atlanta and operate the Hawks. He has indicated that he will do so.

Ben Kerner

107

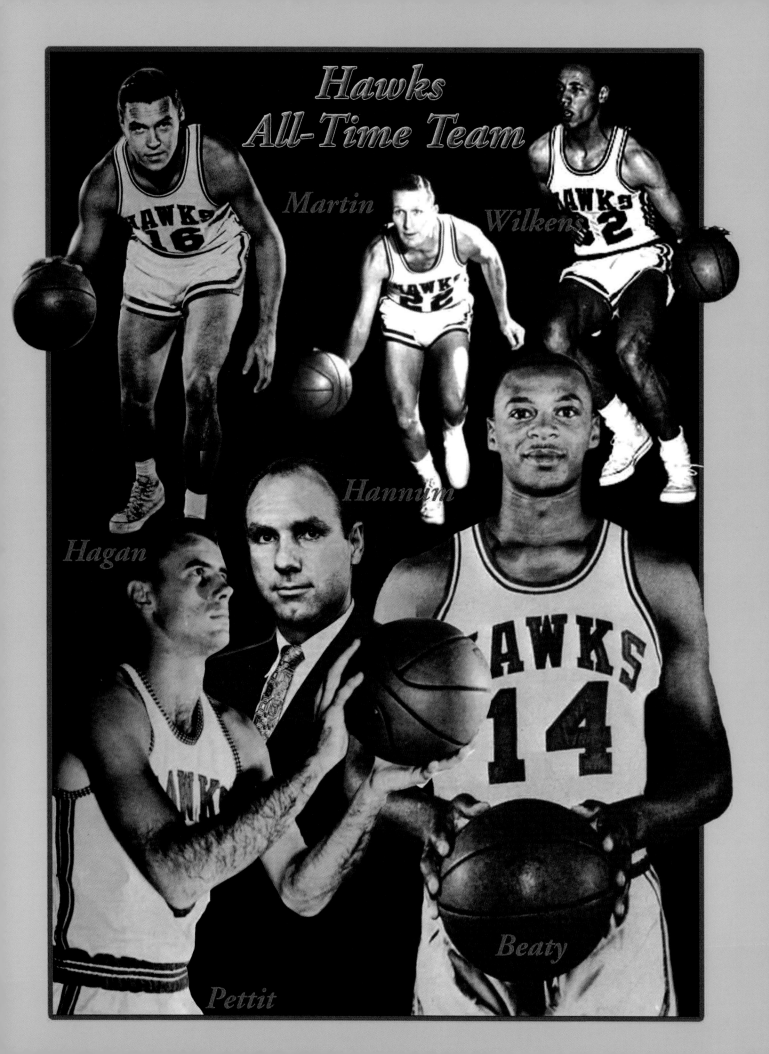

Hawks
All-Time Team

Martin

Wilkens

Hannum

Hagan

Pettit

Beaty

12 THE HAWKS' ALL-TIME STARTING FIVE

Ready for some arguments? This is not brain surgery, and there's no special formula. After some conversations with the men who played and the fans who watched, I reached these conclusions about the Hawks all-time teams. Agree or disagree with the list, one thing is for sure—this team of seven Hall-of-Famers could surely compete with any team of its era. By the way, there was a time when four of the starting five here did play together.

The Guards
Slater Martin
Lenny Wilkens

The Forwards
Bob Pettit
Cliff Hagan

The Center
Zelmo Beaty

The Coach
Alex Hannum

The All-Time Roster

**Charlie Share, Clyde Lovellette, Ed Macauley,
Bill Bridges, Richie Guerin, Lou Hudson, Joe Caldwell**

13 THE INCOMPARABLE NO. 9, BOB PETTIT

He was one of the most dominant players in the history of professional basketball. Bob Pettit was the best forward if not the best player of his era, and he symbolized the Hawks for the first ten years of their stay in St. Louis.

The greatest coach in NBA history, Boston's Arnold Red Auerbach, expressed the ultimate compliment to the greatest Hawk: "In his day, Pettit was the best power forward in the game," said Red. "Pettit could do more things than the others because he could play some center and was a much stronger rebounder. Pettit was Mr. Clean, Mr. All America. He was a clean liver and a super guy, but very, very competitive. Whether he was 50 points ahead or behind, it didn't matter."

Pettit had the seldom-seen ability to play inside or outside depending on the opponent. His patented jump shot, his one-handed push shot, an occasional hook shot, a drive for the basket, and his unmistakable second effort were the products of this superstar. That drive to succeed left him never completely satisfied.

Drafted in the summer of 1954 by the Milwaukee Hawks, he played immediately for the last-place

AMADEE

club, which helped his fast transition into the speed and style of the pro game. Pettit's impact was immediate and profound: How about being both the NBA Rookie of the Year and First Team All-Pro the same season?

Big Blue fought through injuries and double-teaming to be an All-Pro performer all 11 seasons he played. Fellow star and Hall-of-Famer Easy Ed Macauley has complete admiration for his teammate and thanks Bob for his championship ring: "I did more watching than playing in that final game in the 1958 NBA Finals. Bob Pettit played one of the greatest games, putting on one of the most clutch performances in a championship setting ever seen to this day in pro sports. Something every athlete dreams about is wearing a championship ring and I know everybody on the team had their contributions that day. But I don't care what anybody else thinks, I'm wearing this championship ring thanks to Bob Pettit."

Bob's 50 points in a deciding championship game still stands today as an NBA Playoff record for most individual points. The rest of the list of his incredible accomplishments need only an exclamation point, not an explanation.

6-9, 215 lbs.
Louisiana State University

First Pick of the 1955 NBA Draft

NICKNAMES

Big Blue
The Bombadier from Baton Rouge

NBA Rookie of the Year: 1955
NBA Most Valuable Player: 1956, 1959
All NBA First Team: 1955–1964
All NBA Second Team: 1965
NBA All-Star Team: 1954–1965

NBA All-Star Game Most Valuable Player
1956, 1958, 1959, 1962

Led the NBA in scoring: 1956, 1959
Led the NBA in rebounding: 1956
Hawks (St. Louis and Atlanta) all-time leading rebounder: 12,849
NBA single-game scoring record for championship-deciding game: 50 points
First NBA player to score 20,000 points in a career
Averaged 26 points and 16 rebounds per game for 11 seasons
St. Louis record for most points in a single game: 57
Once had 39 rebounds in NBA game
Selected to the 25th and 35th anniversary All-Time NBA Team
Selected as one of 50 greatest players in NBA history
Inducted into the Naismith Basketball Hall of Fame in 1989

14 PROGRAMS, UNIFORMS, AND OTHER MEMORABILIA

In the days of the Hawks, memorabilia was not a business, and souvenirs were far less plentiful. That's why the value of what many people think are meaningless trinkets are bought and sold for such high prices on the sports memorabilia market.

There are not tons of items in the attics and basement boxes of baby boomers and their parents, but the articles that have popped out of the woodwork seem priceless. There are table lighters with the Hawks logo, rulers with players' faces, ash trays bearing the heads of the World Champions, pennants that say "World Champions of Professional Basketball," and beer glasses with players and logos attached.

The game programs of home games at Kiel are unique. Unlike today's bland pro sports programs that often don't change covers game to game, the Hawks' programs are wonderful historical pieces of those times in St. Louis. On the internet, a "Bob Pettit 1958–59" game program cover, for instance, can be valued at 400 times or more what was paid at the gate!

How about the value of those rare 1950s Topps set basketball cards? Those penny cards in the 1950s of Pettit, Martin, and Hagan can go for up to $200 per card! Try $700 to win an auction of the world championship season felt wall pennant that sold for 75 cents in the concession stand in 1959! Don't even get into the price of an autographed basketball or official team jersey if one can be found.

The Hawks' uniforms are very rare, as players turned them in after the season in most cases. A few jerseys and warm-up jackets have been spotted or owned by team members. Over the years in St. Louis, the Hawks stuck with their basic red and white colors–white at home and brilliant red with white trim on the road.

The exception was the last couple of seasons when someone decided to put the traveling Hawks into a "royal blue" uniform with a little red trim, which frankly didn't look like the Hawks. The best of all was the original 1950s home white with that red, white, and blue trim on the jersey and pants.

Anyway, these are the trimmings that remain the memories of the St. Louis Hawks for their thousands of fans. Don't just hand over those sets of Topps cards or table lighters for nothing to those kids and grandkids! At least not without them knowing their true meaning and value to the franchise's history.

Choice Of The Hawks

Bob Pettit

ST. LOUIS HAWKS
Professional basketball's Number One Player! Leading scorer in the National Basketball Association during the 1955-56 season, Pettit was named to play on the All-Star team and won the title of "Most Valuable Player". An All American at Louisiana State University in 1954.

Team-Tailored BASKETBALL UNIFORMS

Rawlings "Team-Tailored" uniforms put the pride of winning into every team . . . brilliant colors stir the spirit of players and fans alike. Professional styling and skillful tailoring guarantee their good looks and custom fit from the season's first game to the last.

Like the St. Louis Hawks, professional, school and college teams everywhere agree that Rawlings basketball uniforms are . . . *"The Finest In The Field!"*

RAWLINGS SPORTING GOODS CO.
ST. LOUIS · LOS ANGELES · DALLAS · CHICAGO

MISSOURI PRINTING & ENGRAVING CO. 3160 EASTON AVE. :: ST. LOUIS, 6, MO.

100 - 98

BOB PETTIT

NATIONAL BASKETBALL ASSOCIATION

THE
ST. LOUIS
HAWKS

OFFICIAL PROGRAM
35¢

Bedtime Story
by Cliff Hagan

Once upon a time there were five big bad giants. They were each seven feet tall. And one was even nine feet tall. All they wanted was to get that little old basketball away from daddy. But, your daddy knows that little old basketball is not just a basketball. It's bread, butter and' milk and everything nice. And no matter how hard those big bad giants try to get the ball away from your daddy, he won't let them.

But one night in Boston those five big giants started chasing me all up and down and around until they had me surrounded. I had to put that basketball through the golden hoop that lays those golden eggs a la **Ben**edict. But, they were getting closer and closer. Their legs and their arms were flying at me, when all of a sudden I hit upon an idea. I called to Whistle-Mouth, the one-eyed referee, and asked for a time out. I rushed for my supplies and took a big, nourishing, energy-building drink of my favorite beverage, and of course you kids know what that is.

With romping new energy, I drove past those big giants. Under their legs and around their out stretched arms I scampered. They chased me with long, pounding strides until I thought the court was going to break apart. With their hot fiery breath on my back, I didn't turn or hesitate. With the basketball firmly in my hand I leaped high like a leopard for the golden hoop. As I sprung they lunged. Then with my little five fingers I gently dropped the ball through the golden hoop as those five raging giants went smashing into the backboard and out of the story on six fouls apiece.

And then, when it was all over, out came a grand golden coach with thousands of golden eggs a la **Ben**edict as a reward for your daddy. And all the little Hagenites lived happily ever after.

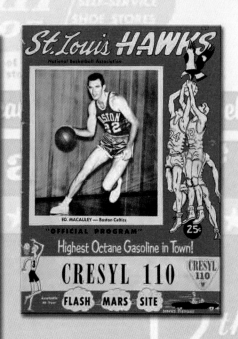

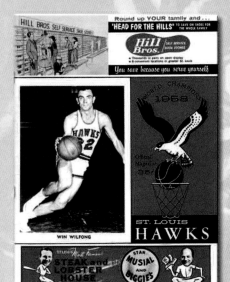

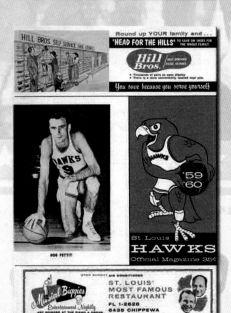

15 ANNOUNCING THE HAWKS

When the 1955–56 season began—the Hawks' first in St. Louis—the public paid little attention to the selection of the first play-by-play broadcaster for the team, whose games would be aired on KXOK Radio 630AM. There was no photo or biography of the new voice of the Hawks in the season press guide. It just simply stated, "Official Broadcaster—Buddy Blattner."

More should have been made of his selection, because Blattner was first a native St. Louisan; second, a former Major League ballplayer with four teams; and third, the current play-by-play voice of the Major League Baseball Game of the Week on the NBC Network with 'Ol Diz, former St. Louis Cardinals Hall-of-Famer Dizzy Dean.

In those days of sports broadcasting, things were done differently, and Buddy had no color commentator—he did the game alone. However, he had a sidekick who would do live commercials between periods and halftime to give Blattner a break from talking.

For the first eight seasons and 800 games, Blattner became as recognized with the Hawks as Harry Caray was with the Cardinals. Except for winning basketball games, nothing had more of an impact on the fans' adoption of this NBA franchise as THEIR TEAM than Blattner. His patented characteristic of nicknaming almost every player and then using it over and over in the course of the broadcast was incredibly entertaining.

The Hawks players celebrate Buddy Blattner's birthday with the cake provided by the home team Los Angeles Lakers after the game in L.A. From left are: Bob Pettit, Clyde Lovellette, Cliff Hagan, Al Ferrari, Lenny Wilkens, Larry Foust, and John McCarthy.

"Big Blue" or the "Bombadier from Baton Rouge," was big Bob Pettit, "Little Abner" Cliff Hagan, "The Old Sarge" Alex Hannum, "Bronco" or "Muggsy" for Al Ferrari, "The Old Rancher," "The Tornado from Texas" Dugie Martin, "Boom Boom" Clyde Lovellette, and "Easy" Ed Macauley were but a few monikers Blattner assigned.

Blattner's smooth but exciting call was the best in the business to St. Louis fans, and he could rile them in with velvety tones when he would say after a bad call went against the Hawks, "Folks, there walkin' the wrong way."

Blattner, who sat high up in the stands in a crow's nest booth with a low-light desk lamp marking his spot to watch from in Kiel Auditorium, became the most important marketing tool of the team. His fast-paced call of the game and colorful characterizations of the men who played drew fans and listeners close to the Hawks. If it could ever be said that an announcer was the "sixth man," the glue of the team, it was the incomparable Buddy Blattner.

When the Hawks moved to the 50,000 "red hot" watts of KMOX Radio, the team and Blattner became a "Midwest and even national team" because basketball fans could pick up the Hawks at night from Montana to Florida. During those first seasons, there were no NBA teams west of St. Louis, so the Hawks were the team in many markets.

The always-innovative owner Ben Kerner became the first to send his broadcaster to every game, at

home and on the road, even in preseason. The other NBA teams did only home games in the early days.

That popularity helped the NBA in another way. Because the Hawks were also a championship-caliber team with several perennial All-Pro players, St. Louis was one of the best attendance draws around the country. Blattner's soothing style was a major contributor to their success.

The broadcast crew got larger in the 1956–57 season when three different color men were rotating through the booth to help Buddy more as a "host" than color man. Their names were Gene Kirby, Bob Crews, and from KMOX, Jim Butler.

Throughout, Blattner kept his baseball job as well, and in fact, the day of the 1958 World Championship game in St. Louis between the Hawks and Celtics, Blattner didn't arrive for the broadcast until midway into the first quarter. He had been doing a Major League telecast in the afternoon and raced back to St. Louis for the sixth game that night. The voice of the game at tipoff was in fact Bob Crews.

By the 1959–60 season, the television games were being done by a man later to become a legendary voice in St. Louis, Jack Buck. He was in just his fifth season as one of the Cardinals baseball announcers, and he would spread his talent to the Hawks' telecasts on KPLR–TV, Channel 11. The team televised 10 to 15 road games.

The same year, a young broadcaster who had been used on some games in the past, Don Cunningham, from WBEN Radio in Buffalo, New York, was on the Hawks broadcasters' list substituting when Blattner was not available.

The 1960–61 season had Blattner and former star guard Dugie Martin doing the TV games, 15 of them on KPLR–TV, while another new man was added, Jerry Gross, a quality basketball broadcaster with an Illinois and Ohio radio background. Gross was also a very polished play-by-play and color man who became popular with the St. Louis audience.

The team of Blattner and Gross split up to do the radio and television of the Hawks for three seasons, giving St. Louis as good of broadcast coverage as there was in all of the National Basketball Association. However, the era of Bud Blattner was ending as the Los Angeles Angels, for whom Buddy had been broadcasting for several years, finally said he could no longer continue as their voice and miss spring training for basketball. The lure of being heard in the Los Angeles market and the size of the job, a 154-game sche-dule plus spring training, was too great to pass up.

For 1963–64, the new radio team was Jerry Gross and recently retired Hawk Al Ferrari. KPLR–TV remained an outlet for 11 games, and NBC Sports was continuing to telecast an NBA Game of the Week, which featured the Hawks several times in the season.

Over the remaining four seasons, Jerry Gross was a constant on the KMOX Radio broadcasts and on television, where a variety of performers filled the color position. Two former stars and Hall of Famers sat behind the television microphone for the Hawks. Cliff Hagan did one season after he retired from the game, the 1966–67 campaign, and in a surprising decision, Hawks management chose one of their bitter rivals, Hall-of-Famer Bill Sharman from the Boston Celtics, to be the television analyst for Hawks telecasts.

The final season in St. Louis saw two more famous broadcasters join the Hawks' list. While Jerry Gross returned to KMOX, the telecasts had the father-son team of Harry Caray on the play-by-play and son Skip Caray on the color commentary. While Harry was in his heyday as the voice of the Cardinals, young Skip was making his mark on KMOX Radio covering the Missouri Tigers, among other duties.

Appendix A

The Hawks Front Office Staff

Owner–President—Ben Kerner
Legal Counsel—Michael Aubuchon
General Manager—Marty Blake
Business Manager—Irv Gack
Director of Ticket Operations—Norm Goette
Director of Public Relations—Bud Cartier
Promotions—Jack Schneider
Team Publicity—Bob Henderson
Box Office Director—Dick Esser
Office Secretary—Jean Bilbery
Assistant P. R. Director—Harold Johnson
Statistical Dept.—Jack Levitt, Jack Brangle,
          Irv Gack
Team Physician—Dr. Stan London
Team Dentist—Dr. Simon Baumgarten
Team Trainers—Bernie Ebert, Kim Tucci,
          John Dunlap

Covering the Hawks

St. Louis Globe-Democrat
Robert L. Burnes—Sports Editor
Bud Theiss—Beat Reporter
Reno Hahn
Charlie Gould

St. Louis Post-Dispatch
Bob Broeg—Sports Editor
Harold Flaschbart—Beat Reporter
John Archibald
Ed Wilks
Bob Morrison

The Sporting News
Lowell Ridenbaugh
C. C. Johnson Spink

East St. Louis Journal
Arnold Irish

Edwardsville Intelligencer
Al Pritzker—Sports Editor

KMOX Radio
Jack Buck
Jim Butler
Bob Holt
Harry Caray
Skip Caray

KSD–TV
Bob Ingham
Howard DeMere

KMOX–TV
Les Carmichael—Sports Director

KPLR–TV
Don Cunningham—Sports Director

KTVI–TV
Jim Brady—News Director

KWK Radio
Gene Davis

KXOK Radio
Bob Shea
Bob Lynn

There were others who worked for or covered the Hawks at one time or another, but this represents the largest group of people who spent significant time around the teams from 1955 to 1968.

Appendix B: Year-by-Year Rosters

1955–56: Charlie Cooper, Al Ferrari, Alex Hannum, Chris Harris, Bob Harrison, Med Park, Bob Pettit, Dick Ricketts, Frank Selvy, Charlie Share, Jack Stephens, Jack Coleman, Jack McMahon, Charles Whiteman, Bob Schafer.

1956–57: Charlie Share, Bob Pettit, Ed Macauley, Jack Coleman, Willie Naulls, Cliff Hagan, Irv Bomoras, Norm Stewart, Med Park, Bob Schafer, Morris Taft, Jack McMahon, Julius McCoy, Jack Stephens, Darrell Floyd, Frank Selvy, John Barber, Joe Gunderman, Dick White, Al Ferrari.

1957–58: Charlie Share, Bob Pettit, Ed Macauley, Dwight Morrison, Jack Coleman, Cliff Hagan, Worthy Patterson, Frank Selvy, Med Park, Win Wilfong, Jack McMahon, Slater Martin.

1958–59: Bob Pettit, Charlie Share, Ed Macauley, Cliff Hagan, Slater Martin, Jack McMahon, Clyde Lovellette, Win Wilfong, Dave Gambee, Al Ferrari, Sihugo Green, Hub Reed.

1959–60: Bob Pettit, Ed Macauley, Cliff Hagan, Slater Martin, Clyde Lovellette, Jack McMahon, Al Ferrari, Dave Gambee, John McCarthy, Sihugo Green, Hub Reed, Bob Ferry, Cal Ramsey, Alan Seiden.

1960–61: Bob Pettit, Cliff Hagan, Al Ferrari, Larry Foust, Sihugo Green, Fred LaCour, Clyde Lovellette, John McCarthy, Dave Piontek, Woody Sauldsberry, Len Wilkens, Stacey Arceneaux

1961–62: Bob Pettit, Cliff Hagan, Clyde Lovellette, Larry Foust, John McCarthy, Al Ferrari, Sihugo Green, Len Wilkens, Woody Sauldsberry, Joe Graboski, Fred LaCour, Cleo Hill, Ron Horn, Rich Eichhorst, Archie Dees, Charles Tyra, Jim Darrow, Bob Sims, Barney Cable.

1962–63: Bob Pettit, Cliff Hagan, Clyde Lovellette, Len Wilkens, Barney Cable, Mike Farmer, John McCarthy, Fred LaCour, Zelmo Beaty, Nick Mantis, John Barnhill, Charley Vaughn, Bob Duffy, Charles Hardnett, Phil Jordan, Nick Mantis.

1963–64: Bob Pettit, Cliff Hagan, Len Wilkens, Mike Farmer, Zelmo Beaty, John Barnhill, Richie Guerin, Bill Bridges, Gene Tormohlen, Charley Vaughn, Bob Duffy, Gerry Ward, Bob "Bevo" Nordmann.

1964–65: Zelmo Beaty, Bill Bridges, Richie Guerin, John Barnhill, Mike Farmer, Cliff Hagan, Billy McGill, Jeff Mullins, Bob Pettit, Paul Silas, Charley Vaughn, Len Wilkens.

1965–66: Zelmo Beaty, Len Wilkens, Richie Guerin, Cliff Hagan, Bill Bridges, Joe Caldwell, Rod Thorn, Jim Washington, Gene Tormohlen, John Barnhill, Jeff Mullins, Charley Vaughn, Paul Silas, Mike 'Farmer, John Tresvant.

1966–67: Richie Guerin, Len Wilkens, Zelmo Beaty, Bill Bridges, Joe Caldwell, Gene Tormohlen, Paul Silas, Lou Hudson, Dick Snyder, Tom Hoover, Lou Hudson, Tom Kron, Rod Thorn.

1967–68: Richie Guerin, Len Wilkens, Zelmo Beaty, Bill Bridges, Joe Caldwell, Gene Tormohlen, Lou Hudson, Paul Silas, Dick Snyder, Jay Miller, Tom Workman, George Lehmann, Jim Davis, Don Ohl.

APPENDIX C: THE FANS REMEMBER THE HAWKS

Thanks to everyone who sent a letter or email about their personal memories of the St. Louis Hawks, and unfortunately space limits the number of fan responses we could use. However, here are the best samples of Hawks memories sent to this author.

"Among the many memories I have of the Hawks includes the basketball camp our St. Mary's High School team attended in the '60s. As Cliff Hagan demonstrated the hook shot, he continuously made shot after shot until he had moved out near what is today the three-point line. Then he said, 'Now if you practice a little, you can go to the other side of the court and use your left hand.' Again shot after shot hit the backboard and swished through the net. We kids were in awe!"

—*Bill Marstall*

"Growing up during the 1960s, the Hawks were a part of my life and led to my love of sports. Bud Blattner, Jerry Gross, and later Skip Caray perked my interest in and actually taught me the game of basketball. Kiel Auditorium was a quaint and special place, from its fabled stage at one end to the baritone tones of Marty Bronson singing the national anthem."

—*Mike Huss*

"My memories are many and they include: Buddy Blattner with his call, 'And they're walkin' the wrong way' after a foul against the Hawks; Slater Martin's underhanded layup style; Cliff Hagan's across-the-lane hook shots; Big Blue's deadly one-handed jump shot; Big Bumper Gene Tormohlen slamming bodies under the boards; and Richie Guerin's two-handed set shot."

—*Ed Bellamy*

"I remember being at a game when Bob Pettit didn't shoot free throws very well. At the conclusion of the game, as the rest of the players left the court, Pettit walked back to the free throw line and began working on his free throws.

"Then when Frank Selvy was in the military service, he could only play on weekends for the Hawks. He would arrive after the game had started, would warm up by dribbling back and forth across the stage behind the basket at Kiel while the game was going on."

—*Dave Silverman*

"My father would always take me to the double-headers, and this time it was the Boston Celtics and the Rochester Royals in the first game. Early in the second period, Boston is up by 20 points so Coach Red Auerbach takes Bob Cousy and Bill Sharman out of the game. I had come to see Cousy and his razzle-dazzle style of ballhandling.

I began to whine loudly to my dad about Cousy not being in the game and we sat right behind the Celtic bench. I guess somebody heard me with Cousy on the bench in the fourth quarter, and Auerbach puts him back in. Cousy does a couple of behind-the-back dribbles, some fancy no-look passes and the lead is up to 30 points. Coach takes him back out of the game, and on his way to the bench he looks right at me and winks! What a thrill!"

—*Kent Wuestling*

"I remember being at the game when the Boston Celtics' Tommy Heinsohn was ejected, and on his way off he gave the finger to the crowd. As he headed up the ramp through the crowd to the dressing room, an older lady seated on the aisle stepped out and whacked him across the head with her purse!"

—*Judge Thomas John*

"I have two memories that stick out in my mind. The first was attending a free clinic the Hawks put on at the Veterans Hospital at Jefferson Barracks. It was in 1957, and I was 15 years old. The players I can remember the instructors were Charlie Share, Jack Coleman, Jack McMahon, and Alex Hannum.

"The second memory was a Sunday afternoon game with my sister. The Hawks played the Detroit Pistons, and the game featured a big fight that necessitated bringing police officers from headquarters down the street. George Yardley of the Pistons started punching Jack McMahon of the Hawks while McMahon was down on all fours. Bob Pettit came flying off the bench with a broken wrist to help, but he was knocked flying by a Piston player. It took a while to separate all the players and restore order on the court."

—*D. Bartz*

"One night in the mid '60s the St. Louis Hawks were playing the Philadelphia '76ers and Wilt Chamberlain. I was 13 and loved basketball. We had good seats near the floor, and the game was great. At halftime, the first player back to the visitors bench was Chamberlain, and my father urged me to ask for his autograph. He wouldn't give it but it was still a thrill to be standing next to the 'Big Dipper.'

"After the Hawks had won the game, Jeff Mullins was the last player to leave the bench, and he gladly signed a piece of paper for me as did the Hawks' owner Ben Kerner said 'tonight, sure, after the victory.'

"After the sixth game of the 1966 Western Conference Finals against the Los Angeles Lakers, a game won by the Hawks to even the series, I ran up to congratulate Coach Richie Guerin. He had no idea who I was but as he walked to the locker room up the ramp he put his arm around me, too exhausted to care. That was the loudest crowd at a game I had ever heard anywhere."

—*Mike Thompson*

"I guess my most bizarre memory of the Hawks was attending a playoff game at the old Washington University Fieldhouse because of a scheduling conflict at Kiel. Another was listening to and watching Harry Caray doing the Hawks telecasts. He was more than just a Hall-of-Fame baseball announcer, and it's a shame people didn't get to hear his tremendous Hawks' broadcasts.

"I can always remember two more things about the Hawks. One was Richie Guerin always making the sign of the cross before shooting free throws. The other was the announcement on May 3, 1968, that the team was moving to Atlanta. On the same night, the St. Louis Blues' Ron Shock scored that famous overtime goal in Game 7 of the National Hockey League Conference Finals against Minnesota to put the Blues in the Stanley Cup Finals in their first season."

—*Scott Simon*

"I was lucky enough to see lots of Hawks games. My recollections include asking 7'0" Swede Halbrook for an autograph; marveling at the ball-handling skills of Boston's Bob Cousy; seeing Wilt Chamberlain score lots of points but also get kicked out of a game; watching two of the best and classiest players of all team really step up in play-off games, Bob Pettit and Cliff Hagan; and watching the tremendous play of the greatest player to ever play at Kiel, Elgin Baylor."

—*Rick Halpern*

"When I was a young boy growing up in Richmond Heights, Mo., I had a newspaper route that included a daily afternoon stop at a lounge called The Floridian. One day, I ran in there to sell newspapers to the patrons and saw two Hawks players, Jack McMahon and Charlie Share. I was star-struck. McMahon smiled, had me sit on a bar stool, and bought me a soda. He asked me if I liked basketball, and I told him I was a big fan and rattled off the names of the players on the team.

"He was impressed and asked me if I wanted some autographs. I said, 'Yes!' He said the next time back in he would bring some for me. I bragged about it to my brothers, dad, and friends, and they all told me not to get my hopes up and that I would never see those autographs. I thought they were right when two weeks turned into months and no autographs. Then the day before school started the next fall I went into the bar to sell papers, and a waitress called me over to the bar. She gave me a huge envelope full of individual signed photos and then a signed team photo of the Hawks. Every one of them was signed 'To Eddie, our no. 1 fan.'

I showed the kids at school who'd been laughing at me, and everyone was amazed they had followed through on the promise. I'll never forget the kindness of McMahon and Share that day. Good ballplayers and great men.

—*Edward Sullivan*

CREDITS

FROM THE AUTHOR

My inspiration to do a second book about the Hawks was the sheer volume of pictures and memorabilia I had access to or accumulated over the years. It gave me a chance in their 50th anniversary year to broaden the scope of Hawks history by including pictures of players and anecdotes about them who were not emphasized in the first book but may have been fan favorites. I had been asked many times at book signings,

"Whatever happened to Zelmo Beaty, Bill Bridges, the Bumper Gene Tormohlen, Joe Caldwell, and so many more. I recognized there still was a thirst

out there for more Hawks information than the first book provided, and I wanted to create a colorful, long-lasting coffee table book to encompass everything that existed in St. Louis about the Hawks.

Thank you to the players and their families who are always available for interviews and who provided personal photos and memorabilia, and to those in the public who answered my pleas for more Hawks memorabilia that we didn't have or didn't know about.

Thanks, too, to my continuing partners at Reedy Press, whose sincere interest in the project and sound advice to me, the novice book writer, got it done timely and with class. Owners Josh Stevens and Matt Heidenry go the extra mile to get it right and have shared my passion for our long-forgotten team. The same can be said for Bill Mathis and Ellie Jones who comprise the design side of the team that has produced this beautiful publication. MathisJones Communications in Eureka, Mo., is known for its top-of-line quality workmanship in publications.

Finally, thanks to my family, who recognizes my desire to finish the task with the Hawks and leave

the public with a complete story in prose and images of our wonderful NBA World Champions. It's important that there are now a pair of books that combine to give the complete story and allows one to visualize what took place those 13 years which began a half-century ago. I want the young sports fans who missed out on watching these exciting teams to be able to understand and appreciate what the Hawks gave to the sports history of St. Louis. To owner Ben, Alex, Jack Mac, the Old Rancher, Med, Walt, and Win from Puxaco, Mo., we remember you for what you gave us on the court for all of posterity.

PHOTO CREDITS

The Naismith Memorial Basketball Hall of Fame; Topps; NBA Photos; Mack Giblin; Jack Zerht Photography; *St. Louis Post-Dispatch; St. Louis Globe-Democrat;* Amadee Wohlschlaeger, former *Post-Dispatch* cartoonist; Ron Jacober from KMOX Radio; William Mathis, memorabilia and the Hawks players family albums.

ADDITIONAL CREDITS

I owe a major debt of gratitude to Bill Mathis and Ellie Jones, who photographed the many memorabilia pieces displayed from a number of Hawks collections in and out of St. Louis, plus their work in restoring pictures from various sites such as the Hawks game program covers. Hawks items have been provided by Dale Radake, Dr. Len Birenbaum, Louis Levy, James Taylor, and those many EBay purchases. Thanks to Karen Klemmer, an executive assistant at KFNS Radio in St. Louis and one of my favorite people, who always gets the job done and done perfectly. And thanks to chief engineer Chris Hoss Nupert, who put together the pieces and the editing for the once-in-a-lifetime CD of interviews and historic play-by-play in the front cover of the book. Finally, thanks to Forrest Langenfeld for providing the Hawks press pass.